SALZBURG

TRAVEL GUIDE 2024

A COMPREHENSIVE GUIDE TO THE CITY OF SALZBURG

CARLTON B. MAYNARD

FORTRESS HOHENSALZBURG

TABLE OF CONTENTS

BONUS MEAL PLANNER JOURNAL/QR CODE

https://eu.docworkspace.com/d/sIH7whaDOAa2wm6wG

SCAN THE CODE ABOVE AND GET YOUR MEAL

PLANNER JOURNAL BONUS FREE

1

INTRODUCTION

Greetings, fellow traveler!

Welcome to Salzburg, where history dances with the present, and each street corner whispers tales of a bygone era. In this guide, we invite you to join us on a journey through the enchanting city of Salzburg in 2024. As you hold this guide, you're not just holding pages; you're holding the key to unlocking the magic that is Salzburg in 2024.

Uncover Salzburg's Allure
Imagine wandering through timeless streets, surrounded by the elegance of Baroque architecture. Salzburg, cradled by the majestic Alps, is more than a destination – it's an immersion into a cultural symphony.

Why Salzburg?

Why choose Salzburg for your escapade? It's a city that seamlessly blends the echoes of Mozart's melodies, the grandeur of medieval fortresses, and the flavors of local cuisine. There's an irresistible charm that makes Salzburg a must-visit in 2024.

Your Guide, Your Ally
Consider this guide your trusted ally, steering you through the city's secrets, showcasing hidden gems, and ensuring you savor every moment. From practical insights to cultural highlights, it's your key to unlocking the essence of Salzburg.

What Lies Ahead
Get ready for captivating landscapes, gastronomic delights, and a cultural tapestry that will leave an indelible mark. Salzburg in 2024 is not just a destination; it's an invitation to create your own unique travel narrative.

Dear reader, turn the page, and let the exploration commence. Salzburg awaits, and your adventure begins now!

Welcome to Salzburg

Greetings, dear traveler, and welcome to the captivating city of Salzburg! Nestled amidst the picturesque landscapes of Austria, Salzburg beckons with open arms, ready to unfold its charm and reveal the wonders that await your exploration.

City of Cultural Splendor
As you step into Salzburg, you enter a realm where history and culture intertwine seamlessly. Be prepared to immerse yourself in the melodies of Mozart, marvel at Baroque architecture, and wander through streets that breathe life into centuries past.

Scenic Beauty and Alpine Majesty
Surrounded by the breathtaking Alps, Salzburg is a visual masterpiece. Majestic mountains provide a stunning backdrop to a city that boasts not only historical grandeur but also natural beauty that will undoubtedly leave you in awe.

Warmth of Salzburg's Welcome
Salzburg isn't just a destination; it's an experience shaped by warm welcomes and friendly faces. Whether you're a culture enthusiast, a history buff, or simply seeking a tranquil escape, Salzburg offers a unique blend of experiences tailored to every visitor.

Your Journey Starts Here
In this guide, we invite you to embark on a journey through Salzburg's enchanting streets, discover hidden

gems, and savor the flavors of its rich cultural tapestry. Let the pages unfold as we navigate this city together, creating memories that will linger long after your visit.

So, welcome to Salzburg – a city that invites you to explore, indulge, and be enchanted. Your adventure starts now!

Brief History of Salzburg

Salzburg has a really interesting past – let's take a quick trip through time!

Roman Beginnings

In the first century, the Romans set up shop here, calling it "salt castle" because people were pretty big on mining salt. It became a bustling spot for trade and mixing cultures.

Archbishops and Churches

Fast forward to the 8th century, and Salzburg became a principality led by archbishops. They got busy building impressive churches and cathedrals, making the city look all fancy.

Mozart's Time

In the late 1700s, a musical genius named Mozart was born here. His tunes put Salzburg on the global map as a music hub, and we still celebrate his legacy today.

Napoleon and Changes
The 1800s brought Napoleon and big changes. Salzburg moved from being a churchy place to part of the Austrian Empire. That meant a shift in how things were run.

20th Century Rollercoaster
The 1900s were a bit of a rollercoaster. Two World Wars shook things up, but Salzburg bounced back. The city showed its strength in rebuilding and even started the famous Salzburg Festival in 1920, putting on awesome cultural shows.

UNESCO High-Five
In 1996, Salzburg's Old Town got a high-five from UNESCO, becoming a World Heritage Site. It's like a badge of honor, saying, "Hey, we're super important historically and culturally!"

So, Salzburg today is this cool mix of ancient vibes and modern city life. When you stroll through its streets, you're basically walking through a living storybook. Cool, right?

Why Visit Salzburg in 2024?

Salzburg in 2024 isn't just a destination; it's an experience waiting to unfold. Here are compelling reasons to pack your bags and make Salzburg your travel highlight this year:

1. Cultural Extravaganza:
    - Immerse yourself in a vibrant tapestry of cultural events, concerts, and festivals that make Salzburg a pulsating hub of artistic expression.

2. Anniversary Bliss:
    - Join in the city's jubilant celebrations as it marks significant anniversaries, adding an extra layer of festivity to your visit.

3. Warm Local Welcome:
    - Experience the renowned hospitality of Salzburg's locals, who are eager to share their city's stories and traditions with a genuine and friendly demeanor.

4. Modern Charms in a Historic Setting:
    - Witness the harmonious blend of tradition and modernity as Salzburg unveils new cafes, street art, and revitalized spaces against a backdrop of timeless history.

5. Alpine Majesty:

- Marvel at the awe-inspiring beauty of the Alps, providing a breathtaking and ever-changing backdrop to the city's enchanting scenery.

6. Unveiling Hidden Treasures:

- Explore newly discovered gems that add an element of surprise to your journey, from cozy cafes to art galleries off the beaten path.

7. Effortless Exploration:

- Navigate the city with ease through efficient public transportation and well-marked pathways, ensuring a seamless and enjoyable exploration of Salzburg's charming streets.

Salzburg in 2024 is more than a snapshot in time; it's an invitation to be part of a living, evolving city that welcomes you with open arms. Come for the celebrations, stay for the culture, and leave with memories that will resonate for years to come. Your adventure in Salzburg awaits!

Franziskanergasse

GETTING TO KNOW SALZBURG

Step into the enchanting embrace of Salzburg, where the air is crisp with Alpine freshness, and each street corner echoes with tales of history and melody.

Salzburg isn't just a city; it's a living masterpiece. Imagine strolling through Baroque streets, a seamless blend of architectural elegance and Mozart's timeless tunes. It's a place where every step feels like a dance through centuries of cultural richness.

While German may be the official language, Salzburg speaks the universal language of hospitality. Locals welcome you with open arms, ready to share not just their city but a piece of its soul.

Picture this: A city that isn't just a dot on the map but a vibrant symphony of experiences. As you navigate its charming streets, you're not just exploring; you're becoming part of a captivating story.

So, get ready to uncover the magic of Salzburg – a place where history meets melody, where culture invites you to dance, and where every moment feels like a timeless adventure. Salzburg isn't just a destination; it's an irresistible invitation to make memories that will linger long after your journey.

Geographical Overview

Alpine Majesty:
Salzburg, nestled in the heart of Austria, boasts a breathtaking backdrop of the Alps. The city is cradled by these majestic mountains, creating a visual symphony of peaks, valleys, and alpine charm.

Riverside Charm:
The Salzach River gracefully winds its way through the city, adding a touch of fluid elegance to Salzburg's geography. This waterway not only divides the historic Old Town from the newer districts but also provides scenic views that enchant visitors.

Urban-Natural Harmony:
Salzburg is a unique blend of urban sophistication and natural beauty. The cityscape seamlessly integrates with its surroundings, offering a picturesque setting where historic architecture coexists with the splendor of the natural landscape.

Living Postcard:
Every corner of Salzburg unfolds like a living postcard, where the geographical features contribute to the city's

undeniable charm. From mountainous horizons to riverside vistas, each turn in Salzburg presents a new and captivating scene.

Gateway to Central Europe:
Situated at the crossroads of Central Europe, Salzburg serves as a gateway to a region rich in history and cultural diversity. Its strategic location adds another layer of significance to the city's geographical presence.

Step into Salzburg, where the geographical canvas is painted with the strokes of nature's grandeur, creating an atmosphere that beckons exploration and promises an immersive experience.

Weather and Best Times to Visit

1. Spring (April to May):
   - Description: Mild temperatures and blooming flowers characterize spring. It's an ideal time for leisurely strolls through Salzburg's charming streets, heralding the city's renewal after winter.
   - Highlights: Pleasant weather, budding greenery, and a prelude to the lively summer season.

2. Summer (June to August):
   - Description: Salzburg comes alive in summer with warm temperatures, longer daylight hours, and a vibrant

atmosphere. The season is perfect for outdoor activities, open-air concerts, and al fresco dining.

   - Highlights: Festive energy, cultural events, and the zenith of Salzburg's vivacity.

3. Autumn (September to October):

   - Description: Autumn brings magical golden hues to Salzburg. Crisp air and thinning crowds make it an ideal time for those seeking a more tranquil experience. The fall foliage adds enchantment to the landscapes.

   - Highlights: Tranquility, golden landscapes, and a touch of magic in the air.

4. Winter (November to February):

   - Description: Winter transforms Salzburg into a fairy tale realm. Twinkling lights, snowy landscapes, and festive holiday markets create a magical atmosphere. Winter sports enthusiasts can indulge in activities in the nearby alpine regions.

   - Highlights: Snowy landscapes, festive ambiance, and opportunities for winter sports.

5. Best Times to Visit:

   - Recommendation: Choosing the best time to visit Salzburg depends on your preferences. If you prefer milder weather and fewer crowds, spring and autumn are ideal. For the vibrancy of festivals and warm evenings, summer is perfect. Winter appeals to those enchanted by snowy landscapes and festive markets.

Salzburg welcomes visitors throughout the year, offering a diverse and captivating experience in each season. Whether you seek the bloom of spring, the warmth of summer, the magic of autumn, or the coziness of winter, Salzburg has a season to suit your travel desires.

Culture and Language

1. Cultural Tapestry:

- Description: Salzburg's culture is a vibrant tapestry woven with the threads of history, music, and art. The city's Baroque architecture, historical landmarks, and annual festivals contribute to a rich cultural experience.

2. Mozart's Melodies:

- Description: The echoes of Mozart's melodies resonate through the city, celebrating the prodigious composer's legacy. From Mozart's Birthplace to music festivals, Salzburg pays homage to its most famous son.

3. Architectural Elegance:

- Description: The cityscape is adorned with Baroque and Gothic architectural gems. Mirabell Palace, Hohensalzburg Fortress, and the charming Old Town showcase the grandeur of Salzburg's historical and artistic heritage.

4. Culinary Traditions:

- Description: Salzburg's culinary scene is a delightful fusion of traditional Austrian flavors and international influences. From hearty local dishes to gourmet experiences, the city invites you on a gastronomic journey.

5. Language Harmony:

- Description: While German is the official language, Salzburg's cultural landscape embraces linguistic diversity. English is widely understood, especially in tourist areas, ensuring smooth communication for international visitors.

6. Festivals and Events:

- Description: Salzburg hosts a plethora of cultural events and festivals throughout the year. The renowned Salzburg Festival, celebrating music and drama, is a highlight, attracting artists and enthusiasts from around the world.

7. Local Traditions:

- Description: Engage with local traditions that add a unique flavor to the Salzburg experience. From traditional folk music to regional customs, these cultural nuances provide insight into the city's identity.

8. Artistic Expression:

- Description: Salzburg is a canvas for artistic expression. Museums, galleries, and street art contribute to a dynamic art scene, reflecting the city's commitment to nurturing creativity.

9. Warmth of Salzburgers:

- Description: The people of Salzburg, known as Salzburgers, embody a warm and welcoming spirit. Their friendliness enhances the cultural experience, creating an atmosphere where visitors feel embraced by the local community.

Salzburg's culture is a harmonious blend of tradition and innovation, inviting visitors to explore its artistic treasures, savor culinary delights, and connect with the heart of Austrian heritage.

ESSENTIAL TRAVEL INFORMATION

Embarking on your journey to Salzburg requires careful consideration of various factors to ensure a smooth and enjoyable experience. First and foremost, check the visa requirements for your specific nationality, as European Union citizens typically do not need a visa. It's essential to confirm that your passport remains valid for the entire duration of your stay.

Understanding the currency and money matters is crucial. The official currency in Salzburg is the Euro (€). ATMs are widely available, and credit cards are commonly accepted in most establishments. To avoid any inconveniences, inform your bank of your travel dates beforehand.

Prioritizing safety is paramount. Be vigilant with your belongings, particularly in crowded areas. Familiarize yourself with local emergency numbers, which can be crucial in unforeseen situations. Carry essential medications and be aware of the locations of medical facilities, ensuring you're prepared for any health-related concerns.

Salzburg boasts excellent healthcare facilities, but having travel insurance is always a prudent choice. Pharmacies are easily accessible throughout the city, and English is commonly spoken, making communication straightforward.

Navigating Salzburg's local transportation is efficient. The city offers a well-connected bus and train network, and a Salzburg Card provides unlimited access to public transport. Salzburg is pedestrian-friendly, allowing for leisurely exploration, and bike rentals are available for those seeking a more active mode of transport.

Language nuances play a role in cultural interactions. While German is the official language, English is widely understood, facilitating communication for international visitors. Learning a few basic German phrases or utilizing translation apps can enhance your experience.

Salzburg operates on Central European Time (CET), so adjusting your schedule accordingly is important. The electrical system operates on 230V, with plug types C and F commonly used. If you're from a region with different standards, ensure you have the appropriate adapters for your electronic devices.

Understanding cultural etiquette contributes to a more immersive experience. Greetings are typically with a nod or handshake, and saying "Guten Tag" for "Good day" is a polite gesture. Tipping is customary, even though a service charge is often included.

In case of emergencies, dial 112 for police, medical, or fire assistance. Salzburg has a dedicated tourist police force, offering additional support and guidance to visitors.

Staying connected is facilitated by the widespread availability of Wi-Fi in hotels, cafes, and public spaces. Obtaining a local SIM card for mobile data is straightforward, and providing your passport may be necessary.

Considering the variable weather conditions in Salzburg, it's essential to check the forecast for your travel dates. Pack accordingly, with comfortable shoes, layered clothing for changing temperatures, and rain gear for unexpected showers.

Before your departure, stay informed about travel advisories and any specific requirements that may be in place. Armed with this essential travel information, you're well-prepared for a memorable and seamless journey to Salzburg. Safe travels!

Visas and Entry Requirements

1. General Overview:
- Begin your Salzburg travel preparations by understanding the general visa and entry requirements.
- Examine the regulations based on your nationality and any specific conditions that may apply.
- Always confirm the validity of your passport to cover the entire duration of your stay.

2. Visa Requirements for EU Citizens:
- If you're a citizen of a European Union (EU) country, explore the nuances of visa requirements.
- EU citizens typically enjoy exemptions, but it's vital to delve into any conditions or exceptions that may be relevant to your specific situation.

3. Non-EU Citizens:
- Non-EU citizens should take a more in-depth look at the requirements for entry into Salzburg.
- This involves understanding the steps for obtaining a visa and preparing the necessary documentation for a seamless entry process.

4. Passport Validity:
- Delve into the critical aspect of passport validity to ensure a smooth entry into Salzburg.

- Consider the expiration dates of your passport and any additional requirements related to its validity.

5. Entry Conditions and Restrictions:
- Be well-informed about any specific entry conditions or restrictions that may be in place.
   - Understand the additional requirements or considerations for entry, providing a comprehensive overview of what to expect upon arrival.

6. Online Resources:
- Leverage the power of online resources to stay updated on the latest visa requirements.
- Explore official websites or dedicated platforms that provide real-time and accurate information, ensuring you have the most current details for your travel preparations.

Embarking on your Salzburg adventure starts with navigating the intricacies of visas and entry requirements. This comprehensive understanding ensures a confident and trouble-free entry into the captivating city.

Currency and Money Matters

1. Local Currency:

- Familiarize yourself with the official currency used in Salzburg, which is the Euro (€).
- Understand the denominations of euro coins and banknotes commonly in circulation.

2. ATMs and Banking Facilities:

- Explore the widespread availability of ATMs in Salzburg for convenient currency withdrawal.
- Assess the accessibility of banking facilities for services such as currency exchange and financial transactions.

3. Credit Card Acceptance:

- Recognize the prevalence of credit card usage in Salzburg.
- Identify the types of credit cards commonly accepted and any potential limitations.

4. Informing Your Bank:

- Take proactive measures by informing your bank about your travel dates.
- Understand the importance of this step to prevent any potential issues with your credit or debit cards while in Salzburg.

5. Currency Exchange Tips:

- If currency exchange is necessary, gather tips on the best places for this service.

- Consider any associated fees or charges when exchanging currency and seek cost-effective options.

6. Budgeting and Expenses:
- Develop a basic budget for your trip, considering accommodation, meals, transportation, and activities.
- Factor in any additional costs or fees associated with currency exchange or credit card usage.

Navigating the currency landscape in Salzburg involves understanding the euro, utilizing ATMs, managing credit card transactions, and planning your budget effectively. These considerations contribute to a seamless financial experience during your stay.

Safety Tips for Tourists

1. Valuables and Personal Belongings:
- Exercise caution with your valuables, including passports, money, and electronics.
- Utilize secure accessories like money belts or anti-theft bags to safeguard your belongings.

2. Emergency Numbers:
- Memorize or keep a record of local emergency numbers, including those for police, medical emergencies, and fire services.

- Program these numbers into your mobile phone for quick access.

3. Health Precautions:

- Carry a small first aid kit with essential medications and medical supplies.

- Familiarize yourself with the locations of nearby medical facilities in case of emergencies.

4. Secure Accommodations:

- Choose accommodations in safe neighborhoods and reputable establishments.

- Follow security measures provided by your accommodation, such as using room safes for valuables.

5. Public Transportation Safety:

- Exercise caution in crowded public transportation areas to prevent pickpocketing.

- Be aware of your surroundings and use reputable transportation services.

6. Tourist Police Assistance:

- Be aware of the availability of tourist police services.

- Tourist police can provide assistance, guidance, and information to visitors.

7. Cultural Sensitivity:

- Respect local customs and cultural norms to ensure a positive interaction with the community.

- Be aware of any specific cultural expectations regarding clothing, behavior, or communication.

8. Communication in Emergencies:

- Learn basic phrases in the local language for emergencies and essential communication.

- Utilize translation apps or carry a phrasebook for ease of communication.

9. Stay Informed:

- Stay updated on local news and any travel advisories for the region.

- Follow guidance from local authorities and adjust your plans accordingly.

10. Group Travel and Safety:

- If traveling in a group, establish a meeting point in case of separation.

- Communicate travel plans within the group and stay together in unfamiliar or crowded areas.

Prioritizing safety during your time in Salzburg involves a combination of vigilance, preparedness, and cultural awareness. By implementing these safety tips, you contribute to a secure and enjoyable travel experience.

TRANSPORTATION OPTIONS

1. Public Transportation:

- Explore Salzburg's efficient and well-connected public transportation system.

- Utilize buses and trains for convenient travel within the city and to nearby regions.

2. Salzburg Card:

- Consider purchasing a Salzburg Card for unlimited access to public transportation.

- Enjoy additional benefits such as free admission to museums and discounts on tours.

3. Walking and Cycling:

- Discover Salzburg's pedestrian-friendly layout, ideal for leisurely walks.

- Rent a bike to explore the city and its surroundings, taking advantage of designated bike paths.

4. Taxis and Rideshare:

- Taxis are readily available throughout Salzburg, offering a convenient mode of transportation.

- Explore rideshare options for flexibility and ease of travel within the city.

5. Rental Cars:
   - Rent a car to explore Salzburg's surrounding areas and the picturesque Austrian countryside.
   - Familiarize yourself with local traffic rules and parking options.

6. Airport Transportation:
   - Arrange transportation from the airport to your accommodation in advance.
   - Consider airport shuttles, taxis, or rideshare services for seamless transfers.

7. Day Tours and Excursions:
   - Join organized day tours to explore attractions beyond Salzburg.
   - Choose from a variety of excursions, including trips to the Alps or nearby historic towns.

8. Trains for Regional Travel:
   - Explore Salzburg's connectivity by train for regional travel.
   - Plan day trips to neighboring cities or scenic landscapes accessible by train.

9. River Cruises:
   - Experience Salzburg from a unique perspective with river cruises along the Salzach River.

- Enjoy scenic views of the city's landmarks while cruising through its waterways.

10. E-Scooters:

- Check for e-scooter services for a fun and eco-friendly way to explore Salzburg.
- Familiarize yourself with designated scooter zones and traffic regulations.

Navigating Salzburg is a diverse experience with a range of transportation options. Whether you prefer public transportation, walking, or exploring the outskirts by car, these choices provide flexibility for your travel preferences.

Navigating Salzburg

Navigating Salzburg is a delightful journey, with various transportation options and a pedestrian-friendly layout. Here's a guide to help you smoothly explore the city:

1. Public Transportation:

Salzburg boasts an efficient public transportation system, including buses and trains. Consider purchasing a Salzburg Card for unlimited access to public transportation, making it easy to explore the city and its surroundings.

2. Walking and Cycling:

Salzburg's city center is pedestrian-friendly, allowing for leisurely walks. Rent a bike to explore the city and take advantage of designated bike paths, offering a unique perspective of Salzburg.

3. Taxis and Rideshare:

Taxis are readily available, providing a convenient mode of transportation. Explore rideshare services for flexibility and ease of travel within the city.

4. Rental Cars:

Renting a car is ideal for exploring Salzburg's surrounding areas and the picturesque Austrian countryside. Familiarize yourself with local traffic rules and parking options for a smooth driving experience.

5. Airport Transportation:

Arrange transportation from the airport to your accommodation in advance. Consider airport shuttles, taxis, or rideshare services for seamless transfers.

6. Day Tours and Excursions:

Join organized day tours to explore attractions beyond Salzburg's city limits. Choose from a variety of excursions, including trips to the Alps or nearby historic towns.

7. Trains for Regional Travel:

Explore Salzburg's regional connectivity by train, allowing for day trips to neighboring cities or scenic landscapes.

8. River Cruises:

Experience Salzburg from a unique perspective with river cruises along the Salzach River. Enjoy scenic views of the city's landmarks while cruising through its waterways.

9. E-Scooters:

Check for e-scooter services, offering a fun and eco-friendly way to explore Salzburg. Familiarize yourself with designated scooter zones and traffic regulations for a safe ride.

Whether you prefer the charm of walking, the convenience of public transportation, or the freedom of driving, Salzburg's diverse transportation options cater to every traveler's preference. Enjoy your journey as you navigate this captivating city!

Getting Around the City

Navigating Salzburg is a seamless and enjoyable experience, thanks to its well-planned infrastructure and various transportation options. Here's a guide on how to get around the city efficiently:

1. Public Transportation:
Salzburg's public transportation system, including buses and trains, is reliable and well-connected. Consider purchasing a Salzburg Card for unlimited access to these services, making it convenient to explore the city and its surroundings.

2. Walking:
Salzburg's city center is designed for pedestrians, making walking an excellent option. Stroll through the charming Old Town, explore hidden alleyways, and discover the city's historic landmarks on foot.

3. Cycling:
Rent a bike to experience Salzburg from a different perspective. The city offers designated bike paths, allowing you to cover more ground and enjoy the picturesque landscapes at your own pace.

4. Taxis:
Taxis are readily available throughout Salzburg and provide a comfortable and convenient mode of transportation. Hail a taxi or find one at designated stands for easy city travel.

5. Rideshare Services:

Explore rideshare options for on-demand and flexible transportation within the city. Utilize popular rideshare apps to conveniently navigate Salzburg.

6. Rental Cars:

If you prefer flexibility and independence, consider renting a car to explore Salzburg and its surrounding areas. Familiarize yourself with local traffic rules and parking options.

7. Airport Transfers:

Arrange transportation from the airport to your accommodation in advance. Choose from airport shuttles, taxis, or rideshare services for a smooth transition to the city.

8. Day Tours and Excursions:

Join organized day tours to explore attractions beyond the city limits. Experience the beauty of the Austrian Alps or visit neighboring towns for a diverse and enriching travel experience.

9. Trains for Regional Travel:

Explore regional destinations by train, taking advantage of Salzburg's well-connected railway network. Plan day trips to nearby cities or picturesque landscapes accessible by train.

10. River Cruises:
   Experience Salzburg's waterways with a river cruise along the Salzach River. Enjoy scenic views of the city's landmarks while leisurely navigating through its water routes.

11. E-Scooters:
   For a fun and eco-friendly way to explore the city, check for e-scooter services. Familiarize yourself with designated scooter zones and traffic regulations for a safe and enjoyable ride.

Whether you choose public transportation, opt for a leisurely walk, or embrace the flexibility of rental cars, Salzburg provides diverse options for getting around the city. Enjoy the convenience and charm as you explore the unique offerings of this Austrian gem.

Useful Maps

To enhance your navigation and exploration of Salzburg, consider utilizing the following useful maps:

1. City Map:
   - Obtain a detailed city map highlighting key landmarks, streets, and neighborhoods.

- Look for information on public transportation routes, major attractions, and notable points of interest.

2. Old Town Walking Map:

- Explore Salzburg's Old Town with a dedicated walking map.
- Identify historic sites, museums, and charming alleys to make the most of your on-foot exploration.

3. Bike Paths Map:

- If you plan to cycle, acquire a map featuring designated bike paths.
- Navigate the city on two wheels, enjoying scenic routes and easy access to various attractions.

4. Public Transportation Map:

- Access a comprehensive public transportation map, including bus and train routes.
- Plan your journeys efficiently, considering the Salzburg Card for unlimited access.

5. Restaurant and Cafe Guide:

- Locate dining options with a map highlighting restaurants and cafes.
- Discover culinary gems and popular eateries across different neighborhoods.

6. Shopping District Map:

- Explore Salzburg's shopping districts with a map showcasing retail areas.
- Find boutiques, souvenir shops, and major shopping streets to indulge in some retail therapy.

7. Hiking Trails Map (if applicable):
- If you're a nature enthusiast, obtain a map of hiking trails in and around Salzburg.
- Discover scenic routes, viewpoints, and nature escapes for a day of outdoor exploration.

8. Museum and Cultural Sites Map:
- Navigate Salzburg's cultural landscape with a map highlighting museums and cultural sites.
- Plan visits to historical landmarks, art galleries, and cultural institutions.

9. Event Calendar Map:
- Stay informed about local events using a map integrated with the city's event calendar.
- Identify venues and locations where festivals, concerts, and cultural events take place.

10. Emergency Services Map:
- For added safety, keep a map indicating the locations of emergency services.
- Note the nearest hospitals, police stations, and other essential services for quick reference.

These useful maps will not only assist you in navigating Salzburg but also enhance your overall experience by providing valuable insights into the city's diverse offerings. Whether you're a history buff, a nature lover, or a culinary adventurer, these maps will guide you through the enchanting streets of Salzburg.

TOP ATTRACTIONS

Salzburg, nestled in the heart of Austria, beckons with a tapestry of history, culture, and natural beauty. Hohensalzburg Fortress stands majestically atop Festungsberg hill, offering panoramic views that echo the city's medieval history.

Mirabell Palace and Gardens showcase Baroque elegance. Stroll through the manicured gardens adorned with sculptures and fountains, and revel in the grandeur of the Marble Hall.

Getreidegasse, a charming Old Town street, invites exploration. Its narrow, medieval architecture hosts boutiques, cafes, and Mozart's birthplace, adding a touch of musical history to the atmosphere.

Mozart's Birthplace, a museum dedicated to the musical prodigy, provides insights into his life. Explore childhood instruments and family memorabilia, immersing yourself in the composer's legacy.

Salzburg Cathedral, a masterpiece of Baroque architecture, offers spiritual grandeur. Marvel at frescoes and the magnificent organ, and absorb the cathedral's artistic and historical significance.

Salzburg Zoo, situated at Hellbrunn Palace, provides a wildlife oasis. Families can enjoy encounters with diverse animals in well-designed habitats.

Hellbrunn Palace and its trick fountains enchant visitors. Explore the palace's architectural marvels and experience playful water features, creating a delightful and engaging visit.

Salzburg Museum, housed in Neue Residenz, is a cultural heritage hub. Exhibits showcase the city's evolution through artifacts, paintings, and multimedia presentations.

St. Peter's Abbey and Cemetery offer a historic sanctuary. Explore the abbey's architecture, stroll through the cemetery, and visit catacombs for insights into Salzburg's religious history.

A Salzach River cruise provides a scenic journey. Enjoy breathtaking views of Salzburg's skyline, including the fortress and riverside landmarks, offering a unique and tranquil perspective of the city.

These top attractions weave together a narrative of cultural richness, architectural beauty, and natural splendor. Salzburg invites you to step into its past and present, creating an unforgettable journey through an

Austrian city that captures the essence of its heritage and charm.

Mirabell Palace and Gardens

Mirabell Palace and Gardens in Salzburg stand as a testament to Baroque elegance, captivating visitors with their timeless beauty.

1. Historical Significance:
- Delve into the rich history of Mirabell Palace, built in 1606 by Archbishop Wolf Dietrich for his beloved mistress. The palace has served various purposes over the centuries, adding layers to its narrative.

2. Architectural Grandeur:
- Marvel at the architectural grandeur of the palace, characterized by its symmetrically aligned façade, ornate details, and the iconic Marble Hall, known for its exquisite stucco work.

3. Manicured Gardens:
- Step into the enchanting Mirabell Gardens, meticulously designed with geometric patterns, sculptures, and vibrant flowerbeds. The gardens offer a serene escape in the heart of the city.

4. Pegasus Fountain:

- Admire the Pegasus Fountain, a focal point in the gardens featuring the mythical winged horse. The fountain is surrounded by allegorical sculptures, adding to the charm of the landscape.

5. Rose Garden:
- Explore the Rose Garden, a fragrant haven with over 4000 rose bushes. The garden's layout and colors create a picturesque setting, making it a favorite spot for visitors and photographers.

6. Sound of Music Connection:
- Discover the Sound of Music connection as the gardens served as the backdrop for the iconic "Do-Re-Mi" scene in the film. The staircase and gardens become a delightful homage to the movie's musical legacy.

7. Events and Concerts:
- Experience cultural events and concerts held in the Marble Hall, adding a dynamic element to the palace. The acoustics and elegant setting make it a favored venue for performances.

8. Accessibility:
- Accessibility is a key feature, allowing visitors to wander freely through the gardens and appreciate the

architectural details of the palace. The site is well-connected, making it easily accessible for tourists.

Mirabell Palace and Gardens, with its blend of history, artistry, and natural beauty, offer a serene and visually captivating experience in the heart of Salzburg. Whether exploring the palace's interiors or strolling through the meticulously designed gardens, visitors are transported to a world of Baroque splendor and timeless charm.

Hohensalzburg Fortress

Dominating the Skyline

Hohensalzburg Fortress, perched proudly atop Festungsberg hill, is a symbol of Salzburg's medieval strength and architectural prowess.

1. Historical Legacy:

- Immerse yourself in the historical legacy of Hohensalzburg Fortress, dating back to its construction in 1077. Initially built to protect the Archbishop's residence, it evolved into a formidable stronghold.

2. Architectural Marvel:

- Marvel at the architectural brilliance of the fortress, showcasing a harmonious blend of Romanesque and Gothic styles. The robust structure and imposing towers exemplify medieval military architecture.

3. Panoramic Views:

- Ascend to the fortress for breathtaking panoramic views of Salzburg and the surrounding Alpine landscapes. The vantage points from its towers provide a stunning perspective of the city.

4. Fortress Museums:

- Explore the various museums within the fortress, such as the Fortress Museum and the Marionette Museum. Uncover artifacts, weaponry, and the history of this imposing structure.

5. Festungsbahn Funicular:

- Access the fortress conveniently by taking the Festungsbahn funicular, offering a scenic ride up the hill. The funicular ride itself provides glimpses of Salzburg's picturesque scenery.

6. Golden Hall:

- Visit the Golden Hall (Goldene Saal), a lavish chamber adorned with golden decor. This grand hall served as a venue for banquets, celebrations, and official functions.

7. Events and Concerts:

- Experience cultural events and concerts held within the fortress walls. The unique atmosphere adds a magical touch to performances, making it a sought-after venue for artistic endeavors.

8. Defensive Features:
   - Discover the fortress's defensive features, including drawbridges, bastions, and towers. The well-preserved defensive structures offer insights into medieval military strategies.

9. Salzburg Bull:
   - Encounter the iconic Salzburg Bull, a mechanical organ with moving figures. This entertaining feature has been delighting visitors since the 17th century.

10. Festungsgastronomie:
      - Enjoy a culinary experience at the fortress's restaurant, Festungsgastronomie. Relish traditional Austrian cuisine while taking in panoramic views of the city below.

Hohensalzburg Fortress, with its commanding presence and historical significance, invites visitors to explore its architecture, immerse themselves in history, and savor the unparalleled views that have stood the test of time.

Mozart's Birthplace

Musical Heritage

Mozart's Birthplace in Salzburg is a haven for music enthusiasts, providing a glimpse into the life and early influences of the legendary composer, Wolfgang Amadeus Mozart.

1. Historical Residence:
- Step into the historical residence where Mozart was born on January 27, 1756. The house, situated in the heart of Salzburg's Old Town, preserves the atmosphere of the 18th century.

2. Childhood Instruments:
- Explore the museum's exhibits showcasing Mozart's childhood instruments, including his violin and clavichord. These artifacts offer a tangible connection to the musical prodigy's early years.

3. Family Memorabilia:
- Discover a rich collection of family memorabilia, including portraits, letters, and personal belongings of the Mozart family. These items provide insights into their daily lives and the cultural milieu of the time.

4. Composer's First Years:
- Wander through the rooms where Mozart spent his early years. Gain an understanding of the environment

that nurtured his musical genius and witness the rooms restored to reflect their original appearance.

5. Sound of Music Connection:

- Uncover the connection between Mozart's Birthplace and the iconic film "The Sound of Music." The courtyard was featured in a scene, adding to the site's cultural significance.

6. Musical Events:

- Experience musical events and concerts held within the historic walls of Mozart's Birthplace. The acoustics and ambiance create an intimate setting for performances, connecting visitors with Mozart's compositions.

7. Salzburg's Cultural Heritage:

- Recognize the birthplace as an integral part of Salzburg's cultural heritage. The site pays homage to the city's rich musical legacy and serves as a pilgrimage for music lovers worldwide.

8. Location in Old Town:

- Appreciate the prime location of Mozart's Birthplace in Salzburg's Old Town. Its proximity to other historic landmarks and attractions makes it a central point for exploring the city's cultural treasures.

Mozart's Birthplace stands as a living testament to the enduring legacy of one of the greatest composers in history. Visitors are transported back in time, experiencing the ambiance of Mozart's formative years and gaining a profound appreciation for his unparalleled contributions to classical music.

Old Town (Altstadt) Exploration

Charming Historic District
Embark on a journey through Salzburg's Old Town (Altstadt), a charming historic district that encapsulates the city's rich cultural heritage and architectural splendor.

1. Medieval Architecture:
   - Immerse yourself in the medieval charm of Old Town, characterized by narrow cobblestone streets, well-preserved townhouses, and architectural gems that transport visitors back in time.

2. Getreidegasse:
   - Stroll along Getreidegasse, the bustling main street of Old Town. Lined with unique shops, charming boutiques, and traditional cafes, it's a hub of activity where history and commerce converge.

3. Mozart's Birthplace:

- Visit Mozart's Birthplace, nestled in Old Town, to explore the historic residence where the musical prodigy Wolfgang Amadeus Mozart was born. The area pays homage to Mozart's legacy.

4. Salzburg Cathedral (Dom zu Salzburg):
- Marvel at the grandeur of Salzburg Cathedral, a prominent landmark in Old Town. The cathedral's Baroque architecture and artistic interiors reflect the city's religious and cultural significance.

5. Residenzplatz:
- Admire Residenzplatz, a spacious square surrounded by historical buildings. The Residenz Fountain and the Residenz Palace add to the grandeur of this central gathering place.

6. Hohensalzburg Fortress Views:
- Enjoy panoramic views of Hohensalzburg Fortress from various vantage points within Old Town. The fortress dominates the skyline, creating a picturesque backdrop to the historic district.

7. DomQuartier:
- Explore the DomQuartier, an ensemble of historic buildings around the cathedral. This cultural and architectural complex includes museums, the cathedral, and the Residenz Palace.

8. Festivals and Events:

- Experience festivals and events held in Old Town, celebrating Salzburg's vibrant cultural scene. The atmosphere is lively, with open-air performances, street art, and cultural celebrations.

9. Hidden Alleys and Courtyards:

- Wander through hidden alleys and discover charming courtyards tucked away in Old Town. These quiet retreats offer a respite from the bustling streets and unveil hidden gems.

10. Culinary Delights:

- Indulge in culinary delights at traditional Austrian eateries, cafes, and charming restaurants scattered throughout Old Town. Savor local specialties while immersing yourself in the enchanting ambiance.

Salzburg's Old Town invites exploration with its enchanting streets, historical landmarks, and cultural vibrancy. Whether you're captivated by its architectural treasures, musical heritage, or culinary offerings, Old Town promises a delightful journey through the heart of this Austrian gem.

DINING AND CULINARY DELIGHTS

Salzburg, a city known for its rich cultural heritage, extends its charm to the realm of dining, offering a culinary experience that mirrors its historical and artistic legacy. As you navigate the cobblestone streets and historic squares, you'll discover a diverse tapestry of flavors that defines Salzburg's gastronomic scene.

The city's restaurants, cafes, and traditional eateries present a delightful fusion of Austrian culinary traditions and international influences. Savory aromas waft through the air, enticing visitors to indulge in the authentic tastes of the region.

Salzburg's Old Town (Altstadt) is a hub of culinary exploration, featuring charming cafes where you can savor a leisurely coffee while taking in the picturesque surroundings. The historic Getreidegasse beckons with its traditional Austrian fare, providing a perfect backdrop for a gastronomic adventure.

Local specialties, such as Schnitzel, Strudel, and hearty stews, grace the menus, showcasing the best of Austrian cuisine. The city's proximity to alpine regions also ensures the availability of fresh and locally sourced ingredients, contributing to the high quality of dishes.

Dining establishments in Salzburg not only cater to traditional tastes but also embrace innovation, with modern twists on classic recipes. The culinary scene reflects the city's commitment to preserving its cultural identity while embracing contemporary influences.

Salzburg's commitment to culinary excellence is further evident in its fine dining establishments, where chefs artfully craft gourmet creations that elevate the dining experience. These venues often boast a blend of international cuisines, reflecting the cosmopolitan nature of the city.

Additionally, the city's annual culinary events and festivals provide a platform for both local and international chefs to showcase their talents. Food enthusiasts can immerse themselves in a world of gastronomic delights, from street food festivals to exclusive dining experiences.

Whether you opt for a cozy cafe in Old Town, a traditional Austrian restaurant, or an upscale fine-dining establishment, Salzburg's culinary offerings promise an exploration of flavors that is as diverse as the city's cultural tapestry. The dining experience in Salzburg is not just a meal; it's a sensory journey that connects you with the essence of this enchanting Austrian city.

Local Cuisine Overview

Salzburg's local cuisine is a delightful blend of traditional Austrian flavors, regional specialties, and international influences. As you embark on a culinary journey through the city, you'll encounter a diverse range of dishes that reflect the rich cultural heritage and gastronomic excellence of the region.

1. Schnitzel:

- A quintessential Austrian dish, Schnitzel is a thinly pounded and breaded veal or pork cutlet. Served with a wedge of lemon, it's a crispy and flavorful favorite among locals and visitors alike.

2. Salzburger Nockerl:

- Indulge in Salzburg's iconic dessert, Salzburger Nockerl. This sweet soufflé, often shaped like the city's three hills, is a light and airy delight dusted with powdered sugar.

3. Mozartkugel:

- Pay homage to the city's musical heritage with Mozartkugel, a chocolate praline named after Wolfgang

Amadeus Mozart. Filled with nougat and marzipan, it's a sweet treat that captures the essence of Salzburg.

4. Kasnocken:

- Enjoy the comfort of Kasnocken, a hearty dish of Austrian dumplings smothered in melted cheese and topped with crispy onions. It's a savory delight that warms the soul.

5. Tafelspitz:

- Dive into Tafelspitz, a classic Austrian boiled beef dish. Served with root vegetables and horseradish, it embodies the country's dedication to simple yet flavorful culinary traditions.

6. Brettljause:

- Experience Brettljause, a traditional Austrian snack platter. Featuring cured meats, cheeses, pickles, and bread, it's a perfect option for those seeking a variety of flavors in a single sitting.

7. Eierschwammerlgulasch:

- During the season, savor Eierschwammerlgulasch, a delicious mushroom goulash made with wild mushrooms known as Eierschwammerl. This dish showcases the abundance of local produce.

8. Alpine Cheeses:

- Explore the variety of Alpine cheeses that grace the menus. From creamy Camembert to tangy Bergkäse, these cheeses highlight the Alpine region's dairy craftsmanship.

9. Beer and Local Brews:

- Accompany your meals with local beers, including Austrian lagers and regional brews. The beer culture in Salzburg adds a refreshing element to the culinary experience.

10. Apple Strudel:

- Conclude your culinary journey with a slice of Apple Strudel. This classic Austrian dessert, featuring layers of flaky pastry filled with spiced apples and raisins, is a sweet note to end your meal.

Salzburg's local cuisine celebrates the city's history, culture, and natural bounty. From savory delights to sweet indulgences, each dish tells a story and invites you to savor the unique flavors of this enchanting Austrian destination.

Must-Try Restaurants

Salzburg's culinary scene boasts a diverse array of restaurants, ranging from traditional Austrian eateries to modern establishments offering innovative gastronomic experiences. Here are some must-try restaurants that showcase the city's rich culinary tapestry:

1. St. Peter Stiftskulinarium:
- Dine in the historic St. Peter Stiftskulinarium, one of the oldest restaurants in Europe. Enjoy Austrian classics in a charming setting near St. Peter's Abbey.

2. M32 Restaurant:
- Elevate your dining experience at M32, located atop the Mönchsberg. Indulge in contemporary Austrian cuisine while enjoying panoramic views of Salzburg's Old Town.

3. Goldener Hirsch Restaurant:
- Immerse yourself in the historic ambiance of Goldener Hirsch Restaurant, located within the Hotel Goldener Hirsch. This restaurant serves traditional Austrian dishes with a touch of sophistication.

4. Zum fidelen Affen:
- Explore Zum fidelen Affen, a cozy restaurant with rustic charm. Known for its hearty Austrian fare, it provides an authentic dining experience in the heart of Old Town.

5. Restaurant Esszimmer:

- Experience culinary artistry at Restaurant Esszimmer, located in the renowned St. Peter Stiftskulinarium. This Michelin-starred restaurant offers innovative dishes crafted with precision and creativity.

6. M32 Brasserie & Bar:

- Enjoy a more casual setting at M32 Brasserie & Bar, located on Mönchsberg. Relish international and Austrian dishes with a modern twist while taking in the stunning city views.

7. Pfefferschiff:

- Venture to nearby Hallwang for a gourmet experience at Pfefferschiff. This restaurant, housed in a historic building, is celebrated for its culinary excellence and seasonal menus.

8. Triangel:

- Discover Triangel, a charming restaurant in Old Town. With a focus on local and seasonal ingredients, Triangel offers a menu that reflects the essence of Salzburg's culinary traditions.

9. Gasthaus Wilder Mann:

- Delight in the ambiance of Gasthaus Wilder Mann, a traditional Austrian inn. Sample regional specialties and immerse yourself in the cozy atmosphere of this historic establishment.

10. Carpe Diem Finest Fingerfood:

- For a unique dining experience, visit Carpe Diem Finest Fingerfood. This restaurant focuses on small, artfully crafted dishes, allowing diners to savor a variety of flavors in each bite.

These must-try restaurants in Salzburg cater to a range of culinary preferences, ensuring that every visitor can embark on a gastronomic journey that reflects the city's diverse and vibrant food scene.

Cafés and Bakeries

Salzburg's café culture is an integral part of its social fabric, offering not just a cup of coffee but a delightful experience immersed in the city's rich history and picturesque surroundings. Here are some charming cafés and bakeries where you can savor the essence of Salzburg:

1. Café Tomaselli:

- Established in 1705, Café Tomaselli is one of the oldest coffee houses in Austria. Located on Alter Markt, it exudes historic charm and serves traditional Austrian pastries.

2. Café Bazar:

- Nestled along the Salzach River, Café Bazar is a classic Viennese-style café. Enjoy a leisurely breakfast or a slice of cake while taking in panoramic views of the river and Hohensalzburg Fortress.

3. Fürst:
- Indulge in the original Mozartkugel at Fürst. This iconic confectionery, founded in 1884, is known for creating the famous Mozart chocolate praline.

4. Afro Café:
- Immerse yourself in a cozy atmosphere at Afro Café. Located in Old Town, it offers a diverse menu of coffee, tea, and delectable cakes.

5. Kaffee Alchemie:
- Experience the art of coffee at Kaffee Alchemie. This specialty coffee shop focuses on high-quality beans and expert brewing techniques, providing a haven for coffee enthusiasts.

6. Fingerlos Café & Confiserie:
- Delight in exquisite pastries and cakes at Fingerlos Café & Confiserie. With its elegant interior, it's a perfect spot to enjoy a sweet treat in a refined setting.

7. 220 Grad:

- For a modern café experience, visit 220 Grad. This trendy coffee shop is dedicated to serving exceptional coffee and features a minimalist design.

8. Strobl:

- Step into Café-Konditorei Strobl for a taste of traditional Austrian pastries. Located near Mirabell Palace, it's an ideal spot to unwind after exploring the nearby attractions.

9. Afro Coffee Salzburg:

- Another gem from Afro Coffee, this branch offers a vibrant ambiance and a menu featuring a variety of coffee blends, teas, and freshly baked goods.

10. Wild & Root:

- Discover Wild & Root, a unique café that emphasizes healthy and organic offerings. Enjoy a range of plant-based treats, smoothie bowls, and artisanal coffee in a relaxed setting.

These cafés and bakeries not only serve exceptional coffee and pastries but also provide a cozy retreat where you can soak in the local atmosphere and appreciate the cultural nuances of Salzburg's café scene.

CULTURAL EXPERIENCES

Salzburg beckons with a tapestry of immersive cultural experiences that invite visitors to delve into the city's rich artistic and historical heritage. The renowned Salzburg Festival stands as a pinnacle of cultural celebration, offering world-class performances in the realms of classical music and the performing arts. Attend a Mozart concert to immerse yourself in the musical genius of the city's most famous composer, or embark on the Sound of Music Tour to explore filming locations and relive the magic of the beloved movie.

The Salzburg Marionette Theatre adds a unique dimension to cultural exploration, presenting enchanting puppetry performances that captivate audiences of all ages. The DomQuartier, encompassing the Salzburg Cathedral and Residenz Palace, serves as a cultural and architectural ensemble where visitors can gain insights into the city's history and artistic evolution.

For a memorable musical experience, consider attending a concert at Hohensalzburg Fortress through the Festungskonzerte series, blending history and music within the fortress walls. The Salzburg Museum in Neue Residenz provides a comprehensive overview of the city's past and present, while the Museum der Moderne Salzburg on Mönchsberg showcases modern and contemporary art against a backdrop of breathtaking views.

Strolling through Old Town, a UNESCO World Heritage Site, offers a glimpse into the architectural charm and historical significance of Salzburg. Explore hidden alleys, visit Mozart's Birthplace, and absorb the cultural richness that permeates the city's oldest district.

The Salzburg Residenz, former residence of the Archbishops, invites visitors to wander through opulent rooms and appreciate the Baroque-era beauty. Beyond formal institutions, Salzburg's local galleries and independent art studios contribute to a dynamic and diverse cultural landscape.

During the holiday season, the enchanting Christmas markets (Advent Markets) showcase festive traditions, crafts, and seasonal delights, adding a touch of magic to the city's winter charm.

These cultural experiences collectively paint a vivid portrait of Salzburg's artistic soul, inviting travelers to partake in the city's classical heritage, cinematic history, and vibrant contemporary cultural expressions.

Salzburg Music and Festivals

Salzburg, a city steeped in musical history, resonates with a vibrant musical culture and hosts renowned festivals that celebrate its rich artistic legacy. From classical compositions to contemporary sounds, Salzburg offers a diverse musical tapestry that captivates enthusiasts from around the world.

The annual **Salzburg Festival** stands as a pinnacle in the world of classical music and performing arts. Established in 1920, the festival attracts top-tier musicians, conductors, and artists to showcase their talents against the backdrop of Salzburg's stunning landscapes. Attendees can revel in opera performances, orchestral concerts, and theatrical productions, creating a harmonious celebration of the arts.

Mozart's legacy is omnipresent in Salzburg, and visitors can immerse themselves in his music through various concerts and performances held throughout the city. Whether attending a Mozart concert in a historic venue or exploring the composer's birthplace, the city provides an enchanting setting to experience the timeless melodies of Wolfgang Amadeus Mozart.

In addition to classical music, Salzburg embraces a dynamic range of genres, attracting music lovers of all tastes. The city hosts events like the **Jazz & The City Festival**, offering a platform for jazz enthusiasts to savor performances in eclectic settings across Salzburg.

For those seeking a more intimate musical experience, the **Salzburg Chamber Music Festival** showcases the brilliance of chamber music in historic venues, creating an atmosphere where audiences can connect with the performers and the music on a deeper level.

Salzburg's musical calendar is also enriched by the **Mozartwoche (Mozart Week)**, a celebration that occurs around Mozart's birthday in late January. The festival features a series of concerts, operas, and events dedicated to Mozart's works, attracting both seasoned classical music aficionados and newcomers.

Beyond formal festivals, the city's vibrant street music scene and impromptu performances contribute to the lively atmosphere. Salzburg's commitment to musical excellence, combined with its picturesque surroundings, creates an unparalleled experience for those seeking to immerse themselves in the harmonies of this Austrian gem.

In Salzburg, music isn't just an art form; it's a cultural treasure that echoes through the city's streets, historic venues, and festival halls, inviting visitors to partake in a symphony of experiences.

Traditional Events

Salzburg, deeply rooted in tradition, hosts a variety of events that reflect the city's rich cultural heritage and celebrate its longstanding customs. These traditional events offer a glimpse into the heart of Salzburg's community spirit and historical legacy.

1. Salzburg Easter Festival:
   - Embrace the festive spirit of Easter at the Salzburg Easter Festival, featuring classical concerts, opera performances, and cultural events. The festival combines musical excellence with the joyous atmosphere of the Easter season.

2. Rupertikirtag:
   - Rupertikirtag, named after the city's patron saint, St. Rupert, is an annual folk fair held in September. The event features traditional music, folk dances, local crafts, and culinary delights, creating a lively atmosphere in Salzburg's Old Town.

3. Perchten Parade:
   - Experience the mystical Perchten Parade during the Christmas season. Masked performers, known as

Perchten, parade through the streets, embodying ancient Alpine traditions and folklore.

4. Advent Markets (Christkindlmarkt):

- The Advent Markets, held in the weeks leading up to Christmas, transform Salzburg into a winter wonderland. These markets, such as the Christkindlmarkt in Residenzplatz, showcase festive decorations, seasonal treats, and handcrafted gifts.

5. Salzburger Dult:

- Join the festivities at the Salzburger Dult, a traditional fair featuring amusement rides, carnival games, and a lively atmosphere. Held twice a year, this event adds a touch of joy to the city's cultural calendar.

6. Corpus Christi Procession:

- Witness the Corpus Christi Procession, a religious event that takes place in June. The procession, featuring clergy, believers, and traditional costumes, moves through the streets, showcasing Salzburg's deep-rooted Christian traditions.

7. St. Rupert's Day (Ruperti Kramperlmarkt):

- Celebrate St. Rupert's Day with the Ruperti Kramperlmarkt, a traditional market held in December. The market features craft stalls, seasonal treats, and folklore performances, creating a festive atmosphere in Salzburg's squares.

8. St. Nicholas Day (Nikolaus Day):

- Experience St. Nicholas Day on December 6th, marked by parades and processions featuring St. Nicholas and his companions. This day is often accompanied by festive events, especially for children.

9. Bauernherbst:

- Immerse yourself in Bauernherbst, or "Farmers' Autumn," a celebration of rural traditions. This event, held in the autumn months, includes harvest festivals, traditional music, and regional culinary delights.

10. Salzburg Advent Singing:

- Enjoy the Salzburg Advent Singing, an annual event featuring traditional Alpine choir performances. The harmonious melodies and festive atmosphere contribute to the city's enchanting Christmas celebrations.

These traditional events in Salzburg provide a wonderful opportunity for both locals and visitors to engage with the city's cultural heritage, partake in age-old customs, and revel in the warmth of community celebrations.

Art and Museums

Salzburg, a city steeped in history and culture, offers a diverse array of museums and art institutions that showcase its rich heritage. From classical art to modern exhibits, visitors can explore the city's artistic legacy through various galleries and cultural spaces.

1. Salzburg Museum (Neue Residenz):

- The Salzburg Museum, housed in Neue Residenz, provides a comprehensive overview of the city's history, art, and cultural evolution. Exhibits span from prehistoric times to the present day, offering a captivating journey through Salzburg's past.

2. Museum der Moderne Salzburg (Mönchsberg):

- Perched on Mönchsberg, the Museum der Moderne Salzburg features modern and contemporary art. The museum's innovative exhibitions, coupled with panoramic views of the city, create a dynamic cultural experience.

3. DomQuartier Salzburg:

- DomQuartier encompasses the Salzburg Cathedral, Residenz Palace, and various museums, offering a cultural and architectural ensemble. Visitors can explore the Residenz Gallery, showcasing European paintings from the 16th to the 19th centuries.

4. Mozart's Birthplace:

- Mozart's Birthplace, a historic house in Getreidegasse, is a pilgrimage site for music enthusiasts. The museum displays Mozart's childhood instruments, family memorabilia, and provides insights into the composer's early years.

5. Haus der Natur:

- Haus der Natur (House of Nature) is a natural history museum that appeals to both children and adults. Interactive exhibits explore topics such as astronomy, biology, and geology, making it an educational and entertaining experience.

6. Panorama Museum:

- The Panorama Museum features the famous Panorama of Salzburg, a circular painting depicting the city in the early 19th century. This immersive artwork provides a unique perspective on Salzburg's historical landscape.

7. Hellbrunn Palace and Trick Fountains:

- Hellbrunn Palace, known for its trick fountains and beautiful gardens, offers a cultural experience. Visitors can explore the palace's art collections and enjoy the whimsical water features in the gardens.

8. Salzburg Baroque Museum:

- Located in the Neue Residenz, the Salzburg Baroque Museum focuses on Baroque art and culture. It showcases artifacts from the Baroque period, including furniture, paintings, and decorative arts.

9. Rupertinum - Museum of Modern and Contemporary Art:

- The Rupertinum houses the Museum of Modern and Contemporary Art in Salzburg. Its diverse collection features works by Austrian and international artists, providing insights into modern art movements.

10. Dommuseum Salzburg:

- Dommuseum Salzburg, adjacent to the Salzburg Cathedral, displays ecclesiastical art and treasures. The museum's collection includes religious artifacts, sculptures, and paintings from different periods.

Exploring Salzburg's art and museums is not just a journey through time but also an immersion into the city's cultural narrative. Each museum and gallery contributes to the vibrant tapestry of Salzburg's artistic identity.

OUTDOOR ADVENTURES

Salzburg beckons outdoor enthusiasts with a plethora of adventures set against the backdrop of its stunning alpine landscapes and pristine lakes. Untersberg Mountain, accessible by cable car or hiking, offers panoramic views of the city and the Alps. Gaisberg Mountain provides opportunities for hiking, mountain biking, and paragliding, rewarding adventurers with breathtaking vistas.

Hohensalzburg Fortress invites history and nature lovers to embark on a scenic hike through lush greenery. The Salzach River Cycling Path provides a picturesque route for cyclists along the riverbanks, while nearby Königssee Lake in Germany offers boat rides amidst the towering mountains of Berchtesgaden National Park.

For water enthusiasts, Wolfgangsee and other alpine lakes near Salzburg offer serene settings for activities such as stand-up paddleboarding and kayaking. Explore the natural beauty of Almbachklamm Gorge with its waterfalls and wooden walkways, or venture underground at the Dürrnberg Salt Mine for a unique subterranean adventure.

Salzburg's green spaces, including Mirabell Gardens and Kapuzinerberg, provide tranquil retreats for leisurely walks and picnics. Additionally, thrill-seekers can experience paragliding in Golling, enjoying breathtaking aerial views of the Salzach Valley.

Whether exploring majestic mountains, gliding on alpine lakes, or discovering hidden gems underground, Salzburg's outdoor adventures offer a perfect blend of nature, history, and adrenaline-pumping activities for every adventurer to enjoy.

Hiking in the Alps

Embarking on a hiking adventure in the Alps surrounding Salzburg is a transformative experience, offering a communion with nature amid majestic peaks and scenic trails. Here's an exploration of the diverse hiking opportunities that await in this alpine wonderland:

1. Untersberg Summit Trail:
   - The Untersberg Summit Trail beckons hikers with its challenging yet rewarding ascent. The panoramic views from the summit showcase Salzburg, the Berchtesgaden Alps, and the Dachstein Massif.

2. Gaisberg Trail:
   - For a more accessible hike, the Gaisberg Trail provides stunning vistas of Salzburg and the Salzach

Valley. The trail is suitable for hikers of various skill levels, promising breathtaking scenery along the way.

3. Hoher Göll:

- Adventurous hikers can tackle the Hoher Göll trail, leading to the summit of this prominent peak. The trek unveils alpine landscapes, glacial valleys, and a sense of accomplishment at the summit.

4. Almenweg 720:

- Almenweg 720 is a delightful trail that takes hikers through alpine meadows and pastures. The route provides a serene escape, allowing hikers to immerse themselves in the natural beauty of the Salzburg Alps.

5. Königssee to Obersee Trail (Germany):

- Just a short drive from Salzburg, the trail from Königssee to Obersee in Germany offers a mesmerizing hike along the shores of pristine lakes with the surrounding Alps as a breathtaking backdrop.

6. Watzmann Traverse:

- The Watzmann Traverse is a challenging multi-day trek for seasoned hikers, encompassing high alpine terrain and panoramic views. It's an immersive experience that requires proper preparation and mountain expertise.

7. Hochkönig Panorama Trail:

- The Hochkönig Panorama Trail encircles the majestic Hochkönig massif, providing hikers with stunning views of the limestone peaks and the surrounding alpine landscape.

8. Rauriser Urwald Trail:

- For those seeking a unique experience, the Rauriser Urwald Trail leads through ancient forest landscapes, offering a glimpse into untouched nature and alpine flora.

9. Tennengebirge Circuit:

- The Tennengebirge Circuit is a multi-day hiking route that takes adventurers through the scenic Tennengebirge mountain range, providing a diverse range of landscapes and alpine vistas.

10. Zeppezauerhaus Trail:

- The Zeppezauerhaus Trail leads to the Zeppezauerhaus mountain hut, offering a picturesque hike through alpine meadows and forests with stunning views of the surrounding peaks.

Hiking in the Alps around Salzburg presents an opportunity to connect with the raw beauty of nature. From challenging summits to leisurely alpine meadows, each trail unfolds a unique chapter of the alpine story, inviting hikers to explore and discover the breathtaking landscapes that define this iconic region.

Salzburg's Lakes

Salzburg is surrounded by picturesque lakes that offer not only stunning landscapes but also a variety of recreational activities. Let's dive into the charm and offerings of these idyllic lakes:

1. Wolfgangsee:

- Nestled between scenic mountains, Wolfgangsee is one of Salzburg's most iconic lakes. Visitors can take boat cruises on the crystal-clear waters, explore charming lakeside villages like St. Wolfgang, and enjoy leisurely walks along the shores.

2. Fuschlsee:

- Fuschlsee captivates with its emerald-green waters and the backdrop of the Salzkammergut Alps. The lake is perfect for swimming, fishing, and paddleboarding. Explore the lakeside trails and visit Fuschl Castle for panoramic views.

3. Mondsee:

- Mondsee, known for its distinctive shape and clear waters, is surrounded by vineyards and orchards. The lakeside town of Mondsee offers a mix of water activities, lakeside promenades, and a visit to the historic Mondsee Abbey.

4. Hintersee:

- Tucked away in the alpine landscape, Hintersee is a tranquil gem. Surrounded by forests and mountains, it's an ideal spot for nature lovers. The lake reflects the beauty of the surrounding peaks, providing a serene escape.

5. Hallstätter See (Hallstatt Lake):

- While Hallstätter See is not directly in Salzburg, it's a short drive away and well worth the visit. Hallstatt, a charming village on the lake's shores, is a UNESCO World Heritage Site known for its beauty and cultural significance.

6. Zeller See (Lake Zell):

- Lake Zell, situated in the Zell am See region, offers a stunning setting with views of the Schmittenhöhe mountain. In addition to water activities, the lakeside promenade is perfect for a leisurely stroll.

7. Wallersee:

- Wallersee, surrounded by meadows and forests, is a peaceful lake near Salzburg. Visitors can enjoy sailing, windsurfing, or simply relax on the lakeside beaches.

8. Mattsee:

- Mattsee is a smaller lake known for its clear waters and recreational opportunities. The lakeside town of Mattsee provides a charming setting for a relaxing day by the water.

9. Obertrumer See:

- Part of the Trumer Seen region, Obertrumer See is known for its birdlife and natural beauty. Explore the lakeside trails and savor the tranquility of this hidden gem.

10. Grabensee:

- Grabensee, another gem in the Salzburg Lake District, offers a peaceful escape. Surrounded by green hills, it's a great spot for a quiet day of swimming and picnicking.

Salzburg's lakes not only showcase the region's natural beauty but also provide a wide range of activities, from water sports and boat trips to lakeside strolls and cultural exploration in charming lakeside villages. Each lake has its unique charm, inviting visitors to immerse themselves in the serene and enchanting atmosphere of Salzburg's aquatic landscapes.

Winter Activities

Salzburg transforms into a winter wonderland during the colder months, offering a plethora of activities that capture the magic of the season. From snowy landscapes to festive markets, here are some delightful winter experiences in Salzburg:

1. Skiing in the Austrian Alps:
    - Hit the slopes in the Austrian Alps, where world-class ski resorts await. Areas like Bad Gastein, Obertauern, and Schladming offer excellent skiing and snowboarding opportunities for enthusiasts of all levels.

2. Christmas Markets (Advent Markets):
    - Immerse yourself in the enchanting atmosphere of Salzburg's Christmas markets. Explore stalls adorned with festive decorations, sip on hot mulled wine, and indulge in local treats amidst the magical ambiance of Residenzplatz, Domplatz, and Mirabell Square.

3. Winter Hiking Trails:
    - Discover the serene beauty of winter landscapes by exploring Salzburg's winter hiking trails. Walk through snow-covered forests and meadows, experiencing the tranquil side of the region.

4. Ice Skating in Mozartplatz:

- Lace up your skates and glide across the ice in the heart of Salzburg. Mozartplatz transforms into a festive ice rink during the winter months, providing a delightful experience for locals and visitors alike.

5. Snowshoeing in Almenwelt Lofer:
- For a unique winter adventure, try snowshoeing in Almenwelt Lofer. Traverse pristine snow-covered landscapes, enjoying the tranquility of the Alpine scenery.

6. Salzburg's Winter Festivals:
- Embrace the cultural side of winter by attending Salzburg's winter festivals. These events often feature concerts, performances, and artistic displays that add a touch of sophistication to the season.

7. Advent Boat Trips on Wolfgangsee:
- Experience the magic of winter from a different perspective with advent boat trips on Wolfgangsee. Cruise across the tranquil lake surrounded by snow-covered mountains while enjoying the festive decorations on the boat.

8. Hintersee Christmas Forest:
- Delight in the charm of the Hintersee Christmas Forest, where a magical atmosphere is created with

twinkling lights, festive decorations, and a hint of holiday cheer. It's a perfect setting for a winter stroll.

9. Thermal Spa Enjoyment in Gastein:

- Warm up and unwind in the thermal spas of Gastein. Relax in the healing waters surrounded by snowy landscapes, combining the therapeutic benefits of the spa with the beauty of winter.

10. Cross-Country Skiing in Ramsau:

- Ramsau, known for its postcard-worthy landscapes, offers excellent cross-country skiing trails. Glide through snow-covered meadows and enjoy the crisp winter air in this idyllic setting.

Whether you're seeking exhilarating outdoor adventures or cozy winter traditions, Salzburg's winter activities provide a perfect blend of festive cheer and natural beauty. From skiing in the Alps to strolling through enchanting Christmas markets, the city offers a winter experience that's both magical and memorable.

SHOPPING IN SALZBURG

Shopping in Salzburg is a delightful experience that combines the charm of historic streets with a diverse array of shops, boutiques, and markets. The city caters to a range of tastes, from luxury goods to traditional Austrian crafts. Here's a glimpse into the shopping scene:

Getreidegasse:
  - The iconic Getreidegasse is Salzburg's most famous shopping street. Lined with historic buildings and wrought-iron signs, it features a mix of international brands, boutique shops, and traditional stores. Explore the cobblestone lanes and discover unique finds in this bustling thoroughfare.

Old Market Square (Alter Markt):
  - The Old Market Square is a hub for local produce, crafts, and souvenirs. The market stalls offer a variety of goods, from handmade gifts to fresh produce. It's an ideal place to immerse yourself in the local culture and find authentic Salzburg treasures.

Linzer Gasse:
  - Linzer Gasse, another charming street, invites shoppers to explore its eclectic mix of shops. From fashion boutiques to specialty stores, it provides a more

relaxed atmosphere compared to Getreidegasse, allowing visitors to enjoy a leisurely shopping experience.

Modern Shopping Centers:

- Salzburg boasts modern shopping centers like Europark and the Forum 1 Mall, where international brands, designer labels, and a range of amenities cater to those looking for a contemporary shopping experience.

Handcrafted Souvenirs:

- For unique souvenirs and traditional Austrian crafts, head to stores specializing in handcrafted goods. These may include woodcarvings, textiles, and intricate items that showcase Salzburg's rich cultural heritage.

Salzburg's Christmas Markets:

- During the holiday season, Salzburg's Christmas markets are a shopper's paradise. The markets, including the Christkindlmarkt in Residenzplatz, offer festive decorations, handcrafted ornaments, and seasonal treats, creating a magical shopping experience.

Traditional Costume Shops:

- Explore traditional costume shops in Salzburg to discover dirndls, lederhosen, and other regional attire. These shops provide an opportunity to embrace Austrian traditions and take home a piece of local culture.

Antique Shops and Galleries:
 - Antique enthusiasts will find pleasure in exploring Salzburg's antique shops and galleries. From vintage finds to unique artworks, these establishments contribute to the city's diverse shopping scene.

Apothecary Shops:
 - Salzburg's historical apothecary shops add a touch of old-world charm to the shopping experience. Some of these establishments date back centuries, offering unique herbal remedies, cosmetics, and fragrances.

Salzburger Mozartkugeln:
 - Don't forget to indulge in Salzburg's famous Mozartkugeln, chocolate truffles named after the city's most famous composer. These sweet treats make for delicious souvenirs and gifts.

Shopping in Salzburg is not just about acquiring goods; it's a journey through history, culture, and craftsmanship. Whether strolling through the historic streets or exploring modern malls, visitors can find a diverse array of items that capture the essence of this enchanting Austrian city.

Markets and Souvenirs

Salzburg's markets are vibrant hubs that offer not only a variety of local products but also a lively atmosphere where visitors can immerse themselves in the city's culture. Here's a closer look at the markets and the unique souvenirs they offer:

1. Christkindlmarkt in Residenzplatz:
 - The Christkindlmarkt in Residenzplatz is Salzburg's iconic Christmas market, enchanting visitors with its festive ambiance. Explore stalls adorned with handcrafted ornaments, seasonal decorations, and traditional treats. The market is a treasure trove for those seeking charming holiday souvenirs.

2. Old Market Square (Alter Markt):
 - The Old Market Square is a bustling marketplace where local vendors showcase their wares. From fresh produce to handmade crafts, it's an ideal spot to find unique souvenirs representing the essence of Salzburg.

3. Grünmarkt (Green Market):
 - The Grünmarkt is a daily market offering fresh produce, regional delicacies, and artisanal goods. Visitors can sample local cheeses, pick up fresh fruits, and explore stands selling handmade products, making it

an authentic experience for those wanting to take home a taste of Salzburg.

4. Easter Market in Residenzplatz:

- During the Easter season, Residenzplatz transforms into a charming Easter market. Here, visitors can find beautifully decorated eggs, traditional Easter crafts, and regional specialties, creating a festive and colorful atmosphere.

5. Handcrafted Souvenirs:

- Numerous stores in Salzburg specialize in handcrafted souvenirs. These may include intricate woodcarvings, locally made textiles, and unique items that showcase the city's rich cultural heritage. Seek out these shops for one-of-a-kind mementos.

6. Traditional Costume Shops:

- Dive into Salzburg's cultural identity by exploring traditional costume shops. These establishments offer a range of items, including dirndls and lederhosen, allowing visitors to embrace Austrian traditions and take home authentic attire.

7. Apothecary Shops:

- Salzburg's historical apothecary shops add a touch of nostalgia to souvenir hunting. Explore these establishments for unique herbal remedies, cosmetics, and fragrances that reflect the city's historical charm.

8. Mozartkugeln:

- No visit to Salzburg is complete without indulging in Mozartkugeln. These iconic chocolate truffles, named after Wolfgang Amadeus Mozart, make for delicious souvenirs. They are widely available in local chocolate shops and make for sweet reminders of your time in the city.

9. Artisanal Crafts in Linzer Gasse:

- Linzer Gasse, a charming street, is home to artisanal shops offering a variety of crafts. From handmade jewelry to artistic creations, this area provides a unique shopping experience for those seeking carefully crafted souvenirs.

10. Antique Shops and Galleries:

- Antique enthusiasts can explore Salzburg's antique shops and galleries. These establishments offer a curated selection of vintage finds, artworks, and collectibles, providing an opportunity to acquire unique and historical souvenirs.

Salzburg's markets and souvenir shops not only cater to a range of tastes but also offer a glimpse into the city's traditions and craftsmanship. Whether you're drawn to festive holiday markets or artisanal boutiques, each shopping experience in Salzburg is a chance to bring home a piece of the city's rich cultural tapestry.

High-End Shopping Districts

Salzburg caters to those with a penchant for luxury and high-end shopping, offering districts where international brands, designer boutiques, and upscale establishments converge. Here are the premier high-end shopping districts in Salzburg:

1. Getreidegasse:
   - Getreidegasse, with its historic charm, hosts a mix of high-end boutiques and renowned international brands. Wander along its cobblestone streets, adorned with wrought-iron signs, to discover luxury fashion, jewelry, and lifestyle stores.

2. Linzer Gasse:
   - Linzer Gasse, in addition to its artisanal charm, features high-end boutiques that cater to discerning shoppers. The street's elegant ambiance complements the exclusive offerings from luxury brands.

3. Goldgasse:
   - Goldgasse, a picturesque alley off Getreidegasse, is home to boutique shops and high-end establishments. It

exudes sophistication and offers a curated selection of upscale fashion, accessories, and lifestyle products.

4. Judengasse:
- Judengasse, located in the heart of the Old Town, features exclusive shops offering designer goods, jewelry, and luxury items. The street's historic setting enhances the overall shopping experience.

5. Forum 1 Mall:
- Forum 1 Mall is a modern shopping center that houses luxury brands, designer labels, and upscale boutiques. It provides a contemporary environment for those seeking a diverse range of high-end products.

6. Europark:
- Europark, one of Salzburg's largest shopping centers, boasts an array of high-end stores alongside popular international brands. The mall's stylish architecture and varied offerings cater to the city's discerning clientele.

7. Alter Markt:
- Alter Markt, while known for its historic market square, also features upscale boutiques and designer shops. The square's surroundings offer a unique blend of tradition and luxury.

8. Boutique Hotels' Surroundings:

- Salzburg's boutique hotels, such as those around the Old Town, often have high-end shopping districts in their vicinity. These areas provide an exclusive shopping experience within the ambiance of upscale accommodations.

9. Luxury Jewelry Shops:

- Salzburg hosts renowned jewelry shops that showcase exquisite pieces. Explore these establishments for unique and finely crafted jewelry items, including Austrian and international designs.

10. Exclusive Art Galleries:

- Salzburg's high-end shopping experience extends to exclusive art galleries. These galleries often feature works by renowned artists, providing an opportunity for art enthusiasts to acquire exceptional pieces.

Salzburg's high-end shopping districts blend seamlessly with the city's rich history and cultural heritage. Whether strolling through the historic streets or exploring modern shopping centers, visitors with a taste for luxury will find an array of options that reflect the city's sophistication and elegance.

Unique Local Finds

Salzburg, with its rich cultural heritage and artisanal traditions, offers a treasure trove of unique local finds that capture the essence of the city. Here are some distinctive items and experiences to discover:

1. Handcrafted Dirndls and Lederhosen:
   - Immerse yourself in Austrian culture by acquiring handcrafted dirndls and lederhosen, traditional attire that reflects the region's heritage. Specialty shops in Salzburg offer unique designs, showcasing skilled craftsmanship.

2. Mozartkugeln from Fürst:
   - While Mozartkugeln are widely available, the original and most authentic ones come from Fürst, the creator of this iconic chocolate treat. Visit Fürst's confectionery to savor and purchase these delectable Mozart-themed pralines.

3. Traditional Austrian Ceramics:
   - Salzburg is known for its exquisite ceramics, often featuring intricate designs and vibrant colors. Look for hand-painted plates, mugs, and decorative items that showcase the artistry of local ceramicists.

4. Local Honey and Alpine Herbs:

- Explore Salzburg's markets for locally sourced honey infused with alpine herbs. These unique blends capture the essence of the region's flora, providing a taste of the Austrian Alps.

5. Original Salzburg Nockerl Mold:
- Salzburg Nockerl is a famous local dessert, and you can bring a piece of this culinary tradition home by purchasing an original Nockerl mold. Crafted from wood or metal, these molds add a touch of Salzburg to your kitchen.

6. Vintage Finds from Antique Shops:
- Delve into Salzburg's history by exploring antique shops that offer a curated selection of vintage items. From old postcards to classic furnishings, these shops provide unique glimpses into the city's past.

7. Austrian Wine and Schnapps:
- Austria is renowned for its wine, and Salzburg offers an opportunity to discover local vineyards. Look for unique Austrian wines, including Grüner Veltliner and Blaufränkisch. Additionally, explore regional schnapps, a traditional fruit brandy.

8. Handmade Wooden Toys:
- Traditional wooden toys are a charming and nostalgic gift option. Seek out local artisans who craft handmade

wooden toys, including dolls, puzzles, and traditional Austrian games.

9. Salzburg-themed Art and Prints:

- Local artists capture the beauty of Salzburg in their artwork. Look for paintings, prints, and illustrations that depict the city's landmarks, landscapes, and cultural scenes.

10. Alpine-Inspired Jewelry:

- Adorn yourself with jewelry inspired by the Austrian Alps. Look for pieces featuring mountain motifs, edelweiss flowers, or other alpine symbols crafted by local jewelers.

11. Heimatwerk Souvenirs:

- Heimatwerk is a cooperative that promotes traditional Austrian crafts. Explore their shop for a variety of locally produced items, including textiles, ceramics, and hand-carved wooden products.

12. Salzburg-themed Literature:

- Discover books, both fiction and non-fiction, that capture the spirit of Salzburg. Look for works by local authors or literature inspired by the city's history and culture.

Exploring Salzburg's unique local finds is a journey into the heart of Austrian craftsmanship and culture. Whether it's traditional attire, artisanal treats, or handmade crafts, these treasures provide lasting reminders of your visit to this enchanting city.

ACCOMMODATION OPTIONS

Salzburg offers a diverse range of accommodation options, from charming boutique hotels in the heart of the Old Town to modern establishments with scenic views of the surrounding Alps. Here's a guide to the various accommodation choices available in the city:

1. Boutique Hotels in the Old Town:
- Immerse yourself in Salzburg's historic charm by choosing a boutique hotel in the Old Town (Altstadt). These establishments often feature unique architecture, personalized service, and proximity to key attractions like Getreidegasse and Mozart's Birthplace.

2. Luxury Hotels:
- For a lavish stay, Salzburg boasts several luxury hotels offering opulent amenities, exquisite dining options, and impeccable service. Some of these establishments provide panoramic views of the city or the Alps, adding to the overall indulgent experience.

3. Boutique Guesthouses:
- Discover the intimate ambiance of boutique guesthouses that blend comfort with a personalized touch. These accommodations may be tucked away in

quieter neighborhoods, providing a cozy and homely atmosphere.

4. Modern Chain Hotels:

- International hotel chains offer modern and well-equipped options for those seeking familiar comforts. Many of these hotels are conveniently located, providing easy access to both the historic sites and contemporary attractions.

5. Family-Run Inns and Bed and Breakfasts:

- Experience Austrian hospitality by staying in family-run inns or bed and breakfasts. These accommodations often offer a warm and welcoming atmosphere, with hosts eager to share local insights and recommendations.

6. Alpine Retreats:

- For those desiring a tranquil escape, consider staying in an alpine retreat on the outskirts of Salzburg. These accommodations offer a serene setting surrounded by nature while still providing easy access to the city.

7. Budget-Friendly Hostels:

- Budget-conscious travelers can opt for hostels in Salzburg, which provide shared accommodation options at affordable rates. Many hostels also offer communal spaces for socializing and shared kitchen facilities.

8. Vacation Rentals and Apartments:

- Enjoy a more independent stay by renting a vacation apartment or home. This option is ideal for those who prefer self-catering and a home-like atmosphere. Various platforms offer a range of properties throughout the city.

9. Wellness and Spa Hotels:

- Relax and rejuvenate in wellness and spa hotels that offer luxurious amenities, including spa facilities, fitness centers, and wellness treatments. These accommodations provide a perfect blend of comfort and self-care.

10. Historic Palaces Turned Hotels:

- Salzburg boasts historic palaces turned into luxurious hotels, allowing guests to experience the grandeur of a bygone era. These establishments often feature period architecture, elegant furnishings, and a sense of regal charm.

11. Conference and Event Hotels:

- If you're visiting Salzburg for business or a conference, consider staying in hotels equipped with conference facilities. These accommodations cater to business travelers with amenities such as meeting rooms and business centers.

12. Eco-Friendly Accommodations:

- For environmentally conscious travelers, Salzburg offers eco-friendly accommodations committed to sustainability. These establishments prioritize green practices, energy efficiency, and responsible tourism.

Choosing the right accommodation in Salzburg depends on your preferences, budget, and the type of experience you seek. Whether it's a romantic retreat, a family-friendly stay, or a solo adventure, Salzburg provides a range of options to suit every traveler's needs.

Hotels and Resorts

Hotel Sacher Salzburg
Location:
Hotel Sacher Salzburg is situated along the banks of the Salzach River, offering a picturesque setting with views of the Old Town. Its central location provides easy access to Salzburg's key attractions, including Mozart's Birthplace and the Salzburg Cathedral.

Overview:
A renowned luxury hotel, Hotel Sacher Salzburg boasts a rich history dating back to 1866. The hotel seamlessly blends tradition with modern comforts, featuring opulent interiors, gourmet dining, and impeccable service. With its iconic red facade, it stands as a symbol of elegance in Salzburg.

Room Types:
- Classic Rooms
- Deluxe Rooms
- Junior Suites
- Executive Suites
- Presidential Suite

Each room is meticulously designed with luxurious furnishings, offering a blend of classic and contemporary styles. Guests can expect comfort, sophistication, and stunning views of the river or the Old Town.

Amenities:
- Gourmet Restaurants (e.g., Restaurant Zirbelzimmer)
- Sacher Spa with Wellness Facilities
- Fitness Center
- Business Center
- Wi-Fi
- Concierge Service
- Room Service

Local Attractions:
- Mozart's Birthplace
- Salzburg Cathedral
- Mirabell Palace and Gardens
- Hohensalzburg Fortress
- Getreidegasse Shopping Street

Booking Details:
-         Website: [Hotel   Sacher
Salzburg](https://www.sacher.com/en/salzburg/)

-                 Contact: [Contact
Page](https://www.sacher.com/en/salzburg/contact/)

Price Range:
Luxury accommodations at Hotel Sacher Salzburg typically range from €400 to €1,500 per night, depending on the room category and season. Prices may vary based on availability, promotions, and special packages.

Villa Verde
Location:
Villa Verde is centrally located near the Mirabell Gardens, offering a quiet retreat within walking distance of Salzburg's historic sites. The hotel's proximity to public transportation provides convenient access to the city's attractions.

Overview:
As a charming boutique guesthouse, Villa Verde provides an intimate and welcoming atmosphere. The hotel's design reflects a blend of Austrian tradition and

modern comforts, creating a cozy environment for guests seeking a more personal experience.

Room Types:
- Standard Double Rooms
- Superior Double Rooms
- Family Rooms
- Suites

Each room at Villa Verde is uniquely decorated, featuring comfortable furnishings and a warm ambiance that complements the hotel's homely atmosphere.

Amenities:
- Garden Courtyard
- Breakfast Room
- Complimentary Wi-Fi
- Concierge Service
- Multilingual Staff
- Pet-Friendly Options

Local Attractions:
- Mirabell Gardens
- Mozart's Birthplace
- Salzburg Old Town
- Salzburg Marionette Theatre
- Makartsteg Bridge

Booking Details:

- Website: [Villa Verde](https://www.villaverde-salzburg.at/en/)

- Contact: [Contact Page](https://www.villaverde-salzburg.at/en/contact/)

Price Range:

Room rates at Villa Verde typically range from €120 to €300 per night, depending on room type and seasonal variations. Special packages and discounts may be available for direct bookings and extended stays. Prices are subject to change based on availability and promotions.

Budget-Friendly Stays

MEININGER Hotel Salzburg City Center
Location:

MEININGER Hotel Salzburg City Center is conveniently located near the Salzburg Hauptbahnhof (main train station), providing easy access to public transportation and the city center. The central location allows guests to explore Salzburg's attractions on a budget.

Overview:

Designed with budget-conscious travelers in mind, MEININGER Hotel Salzburg City Center offers a contemporary and functional stay. The hotel's modern design and communal spaces create a vibrant atmosphere, making it a popular choice for backpackers, families, and budget travelers.

Room Types:
- Classic Single Rooms
- Standard Twin Rooms
- Multibed Rooms (Dormitories)
- Private Family Rooms

MEININGER provides flexible accommodation options to suit various preferences and budget constraints, making it an ideal choice for those seeking affordable stays.

Amenities:
- Guest Kitchen
- Game Zone
- Lounge Area
- 24/7 Reception
- Bicycle Rental
- Wi-Fi
- Laundry Facilities

Local Attractions:

- Mirabell Gardens
- Hohensalzburg Fortress
- Mozart's Birthplace
- Getreidegasse Shopping Street
- Salzburg Cathedral

Booking Details:
- Website: [MEININGER Hotel Salzburg City Center](https://www.meininger-hotels.com/en/hotels/salzburg/)

- Contact: [Contact Page](https://www.meininger-hotels.com/en/contact/)

Price Range:
Room rates at MEININGER Hotel Salzburg City Center typically range from €60 to €150 per night, depending on room type and availability. The hotel often offers budget-friendly promotions, group discounts, and special rates for direct bookings.

YoHo - International Youth Hostel

Location:
YoHo - International Youth Hostel is situated near the Salzburg Hauptbahnhof, providing a convenient base for budget travelers exploring the city. Its proximity to

public transportation makes it easy to reach Salzburg's attractions and beyond.

Overview:
Catering to a youthful and vibrant crowd, YoHo - International Youth Hostel offers budget-friendly accommodations with a social atmosphere. The hostel's communal spaces and shared facilities make it an ideal choice for solo travelers, backpackers, and groups on a budget.

Room Types:
- Dormitory Beds (Shared)
- Private Twin and Triple Rooms

YoHo provides simple yet comfortable accommodations, allowing guests to focus on their Salzburg experience without breaking the bank.

Amenities:
- Common Room
- Self-Catering Kitchen
- 24/7 Reception
- Wi-Fi
- Laundry Facilities
- Lockers
- Bicycle Rental

Local Attractions:
- Mirabell Gardens
- Salzburg Old Town
- Makartsteg Bridge
- Salzburg Marionette Theatre
- Mozart's Birthplace

Booking Details:
- Website: [YoHo - International Youth Hostel](https://www.yoho.at/en/salzburg/)

- Contact: [Contact Page](https://www.yoho.at/en/salzburg/contact/)

Price Range:
Dormitory beds at YoHo - International Youth Hostel typically range from €20 to €40 per night, while private rooms range from €60 to €120. Prices may vary based on room type, availability, and special promotions. The hostel often offers affordable group rates and discounts for direct bookings.

Charming Bed and Breakfasts

Villa Verde Bed and Breakfast
Location:

Villa Verde Bed and Breakfast is centrally located near the Mirabell Gardens, offering a quiet and charming retreat within easy reach of Salzburg's main attractions. Its proximity to public transportation and key landmarks makes it an ideal choice for those seeking a cozy bed and breakfast experience.

Overview:
Villa Verde is a boutique guesthouse that provides an intimate and welcoming atmosphere. The bed and breakfast concept allows guests to enjoy personalized service, a homely ambiance, and unique touches that enhance their Salzburg experience.

Room Types:
- Standard Double Rooms
- Superior Double Rooms
- Family Rooms
- Suites

Each room at Villa Verde is individually designed, reflecting a blend of Austrian tradition and modern comfort. The cozy and elegant interiors create a warm and inviting retreat.

Amenities:
- Garden Courtyard
- Breakfast Room

- Complimentary Wi-Fi
- Concierge Service
- Multilingual Staff
- Pet-Friendly Options

Local Attractions:
- Mirabell Gardens
- Mozart's Birthplace
- Salzburg Old Town
- Salzburg Marionette Theatre
- Makartsteg Bridge

Booking Details:
-      Website: [Villa   Verde   Bed   and
Breakfast](https://www.villaverde-salzburg.at/en/)

-                          Contact: [Contact
Page](https://www.villaverde-salzburg.at/en/contact/)

Price Range:
Room rates at Villa Verde Bed and Breakfast typically range from €120 to €300 per night, depending on room type and seasonal variations. Special packages and discounts may be available for direct bookings and extended stays.

The Mozart 22 Bed & Breakfast
Location:
The Mozart 22 Bed & Breakfast is centrally located in Salzburg, just a short walk from the Old Town and key attractions. Its convenient location allows guests to explore the city's cultural and historical landmarks with ease.

Overview:
The Mozart 22 Bed & Breakfast offers a charming and intimate atmosphere, combining Austrian hospitality with modern comfort. The bed and breakfast setting provides a personalized experience, making guests feel at home in the heart of Salzburg.

Room Types:
- Double Rooms
- Family Rooms
- Apartments with Kitchenettes

Each room at The Mozart 22 is thoughtfully decorated, featuring comfortable furnishings and unique touches that add to the overall charm of the bed and breakfast.

Amenities:
- Breakfast Room
- Garden Terrace
- Complimentary Wi-Fi

- Tea and Coffee Facilities
- Tour Assistance
- Luggage Storage

Local Attractions:
- Mozart's Birthplace
- Salzburg Cathedral
- Hohensalzburg Fortress
- Mirabell Gardens
- Getreidegasse Shopping Street

Booking Details:
-    Website: [The   Mozart   22   Bed   &
Breakfast](https://www.mozart22.com/)

-                      Contact: [Contact
Page](https://www.mozart22.com/contact/)

Price Range:
Room rates at The Mozart 22 Bed & Breakfast typically
range from €90 to €200 per night, depending on room
type and season. The bed and breakfast may offer special
rates for direct bookings and longer stays. Prices are
subject to change based on availability and promotions.

ENTERTAINMENT AND NIGHTLIFE

Salzburg's entertainment and nightlife scene offer a dynamic mix of cultural experiences and contemporary vibes. Dive into the city's rich musical heritage with classical concerts and operas hosted at iconic venues like the Mozarteum and during the Salzburg Festival. For jazz enthusiasts, Jazzit provides an intimate space for diverse jazz performances.

Rockhouse Salzburg stands out as a live music venue, presenting a spectrum of genres for music lovers. ARGEkultur contributes to the city's cultural diversity, hosting concerts, theater performances, and art exhibitions. O'Malley's Irish Pub and Shamrock Irish Pub provide lively atmospheres, featuring live music and Irish charm.

Republic Café Salzburg caters to a multifaceted crowd, transforming from a trendy café to a nightclub with live DJ sets and themed parties. Hangar-7 at Salzburg Airport offers not only an aviation experience but also a unique venue for dining and entertainment. M32, perched on the Mönchsberg, provides a sophisticated setting with panoramic views for enjoying cocktails and live DJ sets.

For those seeking a traditional Austrian experience, Altstadt Keller, a charming wine cellar in the Old Town, offers live folk music, hearty cuisine, and regional wines. Club Take Five is a well-established nightclub, known for its vibrant atmosphere and diverse music selection.

Casino Salzburg, housed within Schloss Klessheim, provides an elegant gaming experience for those feeling lucky. The city's nightlife caters to various tastes, ensuring that Salzburg comes alive after dark with a harmonious blend of cultural richness and contemporary excitement.

Bars and Pubs

Salzburg's nightlife boasts an array of bars and pubs that cater to different tastes, providing a social and lively atmosphere. Whether you're looking for a cozy pub, a trendy bar, or a place to enjoy local beers, Salzburg has options to suit every preference.

1. Augustiner Bräu:
   - Augustiner Bräu, one of the city's oldest breweries, offers a unique beer hall experience. Visitors can enjoy freshly brewed beer from wooden barrels in a traditional setting. The beer garden provides a relaxed atmosphere for socializing.

2. Müllner Bräu:

- Müllner Bräu is a popular beer garden with a rich history. This traditional brewery serves a variety of local beers and hearty Austrian dishes. The outdoor seating area is perfect for enjoying a drink in a convivial atmosphere.

3. Die Weisse:

- Die Weisse is a charming brewery and beer garden known for its selection of house-brewed beers. With a laid-back ambiance and a spacious outdoor area, it's an ideal spot to unwind with friends.

4. The Old Irish Bar:

- The Old Irish Bar offers an authentic Irish pub experience in the heart of Salzburg. With a wide selection of Irish and international beers, live music, and a welcoming atmosphere, it's a favorite for those seeking a lively pub setting.

5. Murphy's Law:

- Murphy's Law, an Irish pub located near the Old Town, attracts both locals and tourists. The pub features a cozy interior, live sports on big screens, and a diverse drink menu, including a variety of Irish whiskeys.

6. Shamrock Irish Pub:

- Shamrock Irish Pub is another popular destination for those looking for an Irish-inspired experience. With live music, a friendly ambiance, and a range of beers on tap, it's a great place to relax and enjoy the evening.

7. Watzmann:
 - Watzmann is a trendy bar with a modern and stylish interior. It offers a diverse cocktail menu, craft beers, and a vibrant atmosphere. The bar is known for its mixologists who craft creative and delicious drinks.

8. BIX Jazzclub:
 - BIX Jazzclub is a jazz bar that provides an intimate setting for live jazz performances. With a cozy interior and a focus on quality music, it's a haven for jazz enthusiasts looking for a more relaxed and sophisticated experience.

9. Arge Beisl:
 - Arge Beisl is a popular pub located in the ARGEkultur complex. With a relaxed vibe, it offers a selection of local and international beers, making it a great spot for pre-concert drinks or a casual evening out.

10. Stiegl-Keller:
 - Stiegl-Keller, situated on the slopes of the Kapuzinerberg, offers a panoramic view of Salzburg. This beer garden serves Stiegl beers and Austrian

specialties, providing a unique drinking experience in a picturesque setting.

Salzburg's bars and pubs invite both locals and visitors to enjoy a diverse range of beverages, from traditional Austrian beers to international favorites. Whether you prefer a historic brewery, a trendy cocktail bar, or a classic Irish pub, the city's nightlife offers options for every taste and mood.

Nightclubs and Entertainment

Salzburg, known for its cultural heritage, also offers vibrant nightclubs and entertainment venues that come alive after dark. From dance floors with energetic beats to sophisticated lounges, the city caters to those seeking a lively and memorable nightlife experience.

1. Club Take Five:
 - Club Take Five is a well-established nightclub featuring a dynamic atmosphere and a diverse music selection. Dance enthusiasts can groove to electronic beats, chart-topping hits, and enjoy a lively and energetic ambiance.

2. Republic Café Salzburg:
 - Republic Café Salzburg stands out as a multifaceted venue, transforming from a trendy café to a nightclub

with live DJ sets and themed parties. Its versatility appeals to those looking for diverse entertainment in a stylish setting.

3. O'Malley's Irish Pub:

- O'Malley's Irish Pub, beyond its traditional Irish charm, transforms into a lively venue with live music and an animated crowd. It provides an engaging atmosphere for those who appreciate a spirited pub experience.

4. Shamrock Irish Pub:

- Shamrock Irish Pub is another popular spot for those seeking a dynamic Irish-inspired atmosphere. Live music, an extensive drink menu, and a friendly ambiance make it an inviting venue for a night out with friends.

5. M32:

- M32, perched on the Mönchsberg, offers a sophisticated setting with panoramic views of Salzburg. This upscale lounge and bar provide an elegant atmosphere for enjoying cocktails, fine wines, and occasional live DJ sets.

6. Hangar-7:

- Hangar-7, located at Salzburg Airport, offers a unique blend of aviation and entertainment. Beyond its renowned aircraft collection, Hangar-7 features a gourmet restaurant, cocktail bar, and occasional live performances.

7. Jazzit:

- Jazzit is not only a jazz venue but also a cultural hub that hosts live concerts and DJ events. The intimate setting makes it a favorite for those seeking a laid-back yet lively night out.

8. The Shakespeare:

- The Shakespeare is a trendy bar and club known for its diverse music playlist and energetic vibe. With stylish interiors and a mix of live performances and DJ sets, it attracts a diverse crowd.

9. ARGEkultur:

- ARGEkultur, while primarily a cultural venue, occasionally transforms into a vibrant space for concerts and DJ nights. The eclectic program caters to different tastes, offering entertainment beyond the conventional nightclub experience.

10. BIX Bar:

- BIX Bar, located within the ARGEkultur complex, serves as both a pre-concert gathering spot and a nightlife venue. With a laid-back atmosphere, it offers a selection of drinks and a space to socialize.

Salzburg's nightclubs and entertainment venues provide diverse experiences, from energetic dance floors to sophisticated lounges. Whether you're into electronic beats, live music, or a chic ambiance, the city's nightlife ensures there's something for everyone to enjoy after sunset.

DAY TRIPS FROM SALZBURG

Salzburg serves as a gateway to a range of captivating day trip destinations, each offering a unique blend of natural beauty, historical significance, and cultural richness. Hallstatt, a UNESCO-listed village, boasts cobblestone streets and stunning lakeside views. Berchtesgaden and the Eagle's Nest, located in Germany, provide a historical journey amid Bavarian Alps scenery. Werfen beckons with the Eisriesenwelt Ice Cave, the largest ice cave globally, showcasing enchanting underground formations.

The Salzkammergut Lakes region invites exploration of crystal-clear lakes like Wolfgangsee, creating a serene escape into nature. Königssee, nestled in the Bavarian Alps, promises a pristine mountain lake experience with boat trips to St. Bartholomew's Church. Golling Waterfall and Bluntautal Valley offer a nature-centric day trip with scenic landscapes. The Hallein Salt Mine provides a fascinating glimpse into Salzburg's salt mining heritage through guided underground tours.

Zell am See, a lakeside town surrounded by mountains, invites leisurely strolls and exploration of its charming ambiance. The Dachstein region unveils intricate ice formations within the Ice Caves, accessible via a cable car journey. The Mauthausen Concentration Camp Memorial offers a somber yet historically significant day trip experience. The Salzburg Lake District, featuring Mattsee, Grabensee, and Obertrumersee, provides a peaceful retreat by the lakes and charming villages.

The iconic Watzmann Mountain, accessible through hiking or a scenic drive, showcases breathtaking vistas within the Berchtesgaden National Park. These day trips allow travelers to immerse themselves in diverse experiences, from cultural heritage to natural wonders, all within reach of Salzburg's enchanting surroundings.

Berchtesgaden and the Eagle's Nest

Morning: Exploring Berchtesgaden

Embark on your day trip from Salzburg to Berchtesgaden in the morning, immersing yourself in the scenic journey through the Bavarian Alps. As you wind through picturesque landscapes, the anticipation builds for the cultural and natural wonders that await.

Arriving in Berchtesgaden, begin your morning with a leisurely exploration of the charming town. Wander through its cobblestone streets, taking in the traditional

Alpine architecture and perhaps stopping at a local café for a coffee or a traditional Bavarian breakfast.

Late Morning: Journey to the Eagle's Nest
Following your exploration of Berchtesgaden, make your way to the Eagle's Nest, perched high in the mountains. The journey itself offers breathtaking views, and as you ascend, the historical significance of the Eagle's Nest comes into focus.

Upon reaching the Eagle's Nest, take the specially designed elevator that travels through the heart of the mountain to reach the summit. Marvel at the architectural feat and delve into the history of this mountaintop retreat, which once hosted high-ranking Nazi officials.

Early Afternoon: Panoramic Views and Exploration
Spend your early afternoon absorbing the panoramic views from the Eagle's Nest. The vast landscapes of the Bavarian Alps and the surrounding valleys unfold before you. Capture the moment with photos, breathe in the mountain air, and appreciate the unique perspective that this historical site provides.

After exploring the Eagle's Nest, descend back to Berchtesgaden for a delightful lunch in one of the local eateries. Enjoy traditional Bavarian dishes or opt for international cuisine, savoring the flavors of the region.

Late Afternoon: Lake Königssee and St. Bartholomew's Church
In the late afternoon, continue your day trip by visiting the nearby Lake Königssee. Experience the tranquility of the pristine lake surrounded by towering mountains. Take a boat trip to St. Bartholomew's Church, an iconic pilgrimage site with its distinctive red onion domes.

Enjoy the peaceful atmosphere of the lake, perhaps taking a leisurely stroll along the shores. The reflections of the mountains on the crystal-clear waters create a serene and picturesque setting.

Evening: Return to Salzburg
As the day winds down, make your way back to Salzburg, reflecting on the cultural and natural wonders experienced during your day trip to Berchtesgaden and the Eagle's Nest. The scenic drive back allows you to appreciate the changing hues of the landscape as the sun begins to set, concluding a day filled with history, breathtaking views, and Alpine charm.

Hallstatt - A UNESCO Gem

Morning: Journey to Hallstatt

Begin your day trip to Hallstatt in the morning, setting out from Salzburg with anticipation for the enchanting UNESCO-listed village that awaits. The journey itself is a scenic delight, with picturesque landscapes and glimpses of the Austrian countryside.

Late Morning: Arrival in Hallstatt
Arrive in Hallstatt, often regarded as one of the most beautiful villages in the world. Take in the postcard-perfect views of the Hallstätter See (Lake Hallstatt) and the surrounding Dachstein Alps. The charming lakeside setting, framed by alpine peaks, creates a mesmerizing backdrop for your exploration.

Midday: Stroll Through Hallstatt
As you delve into the heart of Hallstatt, stroll through its narrow streets adorned with historic Alpine houses. Discover the central market square, where you can find quaint shops, cafes, and the iconic Evangelical Church. The peaceful ambiance of the village invites you to immerse yourself in its unique atmosphere.

Early Afternoon: Visit the Hallstatt Salt Mine
In the early afternoon, embark on a visit to the Hallstatt Salt Mine, a significant part of the village's history. Explore the underground world of salt mining through guided tours, discovering ancient tunnels, subterranean

lakes, and learning about the rich salt mining heritage that dates back thousands of years.

Late Afternoon: Boat Trip on Lake Hallstatt

As the day progresses, take a leisurely boat trip on Lake Hallstatt. Enjoy the tranquility of the lake surrounded by towering mountains. The boat ride offers panoramic views of Hallstatt and allows you to appreciate the village from a different perspective.

Evening: Lakeside Dining and Reflection

Conclude your day trip with a lakeside dining experience in one of Hallstatt's charming restaurants. Savor Austrian cuisine while overlooking the serene waters of Lake Hallstatt. The evening atmosphere, with the village illuminated by soft lights, creates a magical setting for reflection.

Nightfall: Return to Salzburg

As night falls, bid farewell to Hallstatt and make your way back to Salzburg. The return journey allows you to reflect on the UNESCO gem you've explored, filled with Alpine charm, history, and the breathtaking beauty of Hallstatt. The memories of this day trip will linger as you journey back to Salzburg.

Sound of Music Tour

Morning: Departure for the Sound of Music Tour
Embark on the Sound of Music Tour from Salzburg in the morning, ready to immerse yourself in the iconic locations featured in the beloved film. The tour promises a delightful blend of stunning landscapes and musical nostalgia.

Late Morning: Mirabell Palace and Gardens
Begin your journey at Mirabell Palace and Gardens, where some of the movie's most memorable scenes were filmed. Stroll through the manicured gardens, marvel at the Pegasus Fountain, and relive the joyous moments from the "Do-Re-Mi" song.

Midday: Leopoldskron Palace
Visit Leopoldskron Palace, the setting for the Von Trapp family home in the film. Admire the picturesque palace and its reflection in the serene lake, capturing the essence of the movie's iconic scenes.

Early Afternoon: Mondsee and St. Michael's Church
Travel to the charming town of Mondsee, where St. Michael's Church served as the backdrop for the movie's wedding scene. Explore the church and its surroundings, reminiscent of the joyous occasion in the Sound of Music.

Late Afternoon: Lake Wolfgang and the Trapp Family Lodge

Head to Lake Wolfgang to visit the Trapp Family Lodge, which inspired the creation of the iconic family home in the film. Enjoy the scenic beauty of the lake and learn more about the real-life Von Trapp family.

Evening: Return to Salzburg

As the day unfolds with musical tales and picturesque landscapes, return to Salzburg in the evening. Reflect on the enchanting Sound of Music Tour, where the hills truly came alive with the sound of music. The memories of this cinematic journey will linger as you conclude your day in Salzburg.

PRACTICAL TIPS FOR TRAVELERS

As you prepare for your trip to Salzburg, consider a few practical tips to enhance your experience. The local currency is the Euro, and credit cards are widely accepted. While German is the official language, English is commonly spoken. Pack weather-appropriate clothing, comfortable shoes, and a reusable water bottle. Salzburg's public transportation is efficient, and the Salzburg Card offers convenient access to attractions.

Respect local customs, show politeness, and be punctual. Tipping is customary in restaurants, usually around 5-10%. Tap water is safe to drink, and safety concerns are minimal, but stay vigilant in crowded areas. Salzburg operates on Central European Time (CET), and emergency numbers are 112 for general emergencies and 122 for police assistance.

Find free Wi-Fi in cafes and public spaces, or consider a local SIM card for connectivity. The standard voltage is 230V with European-style two-pin plugs. Check the local event calendar for festivals, and be mindful of limited store hours on Sundays and holidays. These simple tips will help you navigate Salzburg smoothly and make the most of your visit.

Language Basics

In Salzburg, German is the official language. However, due to its status as a popular tourist destination, English is widely spoken, especially in areas frequented by visitors. While many locals are fluent in English, it can be appreciated if you learn a few basic German phrases to enhance your interactions and show cultural respect. Here are some language basics:

Greetings:
- Hello - Hallo
- Good morning - Guten Morgen
- Good afternoon - Guten Tag
- Good evening - Guten Abend
- Goodbye - Auf Wiedersehen

Common Phrases:
- Yes - Ja
- No - Nein
- Please - Bitte
- Thank you - Danke
- Excuse me - Entschuldigung
- I'm sorry - Es tut mir leid
- You're welcome - Bitte schön

Numbers:
- One - Eins

- Two - Zwei
- Three - Drei
- Four - Vier
- Five - Fünf

Basic Questions:
- What is your name? - Wie ist Ihr Name?
- My name is... - Ich heiße...
- How are you? - Wie geht es Ihnen?
- Where is...? - Wo ist...?
- How much does this cost? - Wie viel kostet das?

Learning and using these basic phrases can enhance your travel experience and contribute to positive interactions with locals in Salzburg.

Local Etiquette

When visiting Salzburg, understanding and respecting local etiquette enhances your experience and fosters positive interactions with the locals. Here are some key aspects of local etiquette in Salzburg:

1. Greetings:
  - Greet people with a handshake, especially in formal settings.
  - Use titles such as "Herr" (Mr.) and "Frau" (Mrs.) when addressing someone formally.

2. Politeness:

- Politeness is highly valued. Use "bitte" (please) and "danke" (thank you) generously.
- Show consideration for others in public spaces, such as giving up your seat on public transport for the elderly or pregnant.

3. Punctuality:

- Being on time is important in Salzburg. Arrive promptly for appointments and meetings.

4. Respect for Quietness:

- Salzburg is known for its peaceful atmosphere. Keep noise levels low, especially in residential areas and public spaces.

5. Dress Code:

- While Salzburg is relatively casual, dressing neatly is appreciated, especially when visiting religious sites or upscale establishments.

6. Table Manners:

- When dining, wait until everyone is served before starting to eat.
- Keep your hands on the table, but not your elbows.

7. Tipping:

- Tipping is customary in restaurants. Rounding up the bill or leaving 5-10% is considered polite.

8. Quiet Sundays:

- Sundays are generally quiet in Salzburg, with limited commercial activities. Respect this by keeping noise levels down.

9. Respecting Personal Space:

- Austrians value personal space. Maintain an appropriate distance when interacting, and avoid standing too close to others.

10. Photography:

- Ask for permission before taking photos of people, especially in intimate or religious settings.

11. Language Etiquette:

- While many locals speak English, making an effort to speak a few basic German phrases is appreciated.

12. Environmental Consciousness:

- Austrians are environmentally conscious. Dispose of your waste properly and participate in recycling efforts.

By embracing these aspects of local etiquette, you'll find that Salzburg's residents respond positively, creating a more enriching and respectful travel experience.

Useful Phrases

1. Greetings and Basics:
- Hello! - Hallo!
- Good morning! - Guten Morgen!
- Good afternoon! - Guten Tag!
- Good evening! - Guten Abend!
- Goodbye! - Auf Wiedersehen!
- Please - Bitte
- Thank you - Danke
- You're welcome - Bitte schön
- Excuse me - Entschuldigung
- Yes - Ja
- No - Nein

2. Common Courtesies:
- How are you? - Wie geht es Ihnen?
- I'm fine, thank you. - Mir geht es gut, danke.
- What is your name? - Wie ist Ihr Name?
- My name is... - Ich heiße...
- Nice to meet you! - Schön, Sie zu treffen!

3. Directions and Transportation:
- Where is...? - Wo ist...?
- How do I get to...? - Wie komme ich zu...?
- Train station - Bahnhof
- Bus station - Bushaltestelle
- Taxi - Taxi

4. Dining Out:
- I would like... - Ich hätte gerne...
- The bill, please. - Die Rechnung, bitte.
- Water - Wasser
- Menu - Speisekarte
- Delicious! - Köstlich!

5. Shopping:
- How much does this cost? - Wie viel kostet das?
- I would like to buy... - Ich würde gerne... kaufen.
- Do you accept credit cards? - Akzeptieren Sie Kreditkarten?

6. Emergency Phrases:
- Help! - Hilfe!
- I need a doctor. - Ich brauche einen Arzt.
- Where is the nearest hospital? - Wo ist das nächste Krankenhaus?

7. Time and Dates:
- What time is it? - Wie spät ist es?
- Today - Heute
- Tomorrow - Morgen
- Yesterday - Gestern

8. Expressing Gratitude:
- Thank you very much! - Vielen Dank!

- I appreciate it. - Ich schätze es.

Feel free to use these phrases during your stay in Salzburg to communicate effectively and connect with the local culture.

Safety and Health

Ensuring your safety and well-being is essential when visiting Salzburg. Here are some safety and health considerations to keep in mind:

General Safety:
1. Salzburg is considered a safe destination, but exercise normal safety precautions. Be aware of your surroundings, especially in crowded areas and tourist spots.
2. Avoid displaying expensive items in public, and keep an eye on your belongings to prevent theft.
3. Emergency services can be reached by dialing 112 for general emergencies and 122 for police assistance.

Health Precautions:
1. Salzburg has a high standard of healthcare. In case of medical emergencies, dial 144 for an ambulance.
2. European Health Insurance Card (EHIC) holders may be eligible for reduced-cost or free emergency healthcare.

3. Ensure you have travel insurance that covers medical expenses and emergency repatriation.

4. Carry any necessary prescription medications in their original packaging, along with a copy of your prescription.

5. Tap water in Salzburg is safe to drink. Stay hydrated, especially during outdoor activities.

Outdoor Safety:

1. If engaging in outdoor activities, be aware of weather conditions and dress appropriately.

2. Follow safety guidelines for activities such as hiking or skiing.

3. In case of emergencies during outdoor activities, dial 140 for mountain rescue.

Transportation Safety:

1. Use reputable transportation services and licensed taxis.

2. Follow traffic rules when crossing streets and use designated pedestrian crossings.

Food and Water Safety:

1. Salzburg maintains high hygiene standards in restaurants and cafes.

2. If you have specific dietary requirements or allergies, communicate them clearly when ordering.

By staying informed and taking necessary precautions, you can enjoy a safe and healthy visit to Salzburg. Always consult local authorities and healthcare providers for the latest information and guidance.

Emergency Contacts

Emergency Contacts:
- General Emergency: 112
- Police: 122
- Medical Emergency/Ambulance: 144
- Fire Department: 122
- Medical Advice (Non-Emergency): 1450
- Poison Control Center: 01 406 43 43
- Lost and Found (Police): 059 133 50 3333
- Roadside Assistance (ÖAMTC): 120
- Tourist Police (Touristenpolizei): +43 662 44 57 70 70

Transportation and Information:
- Public Transport Information: +43 662 19449 (Salzburg Verkehrsbetriebe)
- Airport Information (Salzburg Airport): +43 662 8580

These numbers cover various emergency situations, non-emergency medical advice, assistance with lost items, and information on transportation. Make sure to keep these contacts readily available for your convenience during your time in Salzburg.

CONCLUSION

As you embark on your journey to Salzburg, you are set to discover a city steeped in history, culture, and natural beauty. From the enchanting streets of the Old Town to the majestic landscapes of the surrounding Alps, Salzburg offers a captivating experience for every traveler.

In this comprehensive travel guide, we've navigated through the city's rich history, shared insights on its top attractions, provided practical tips for a seamless visit, and outlined essential information for your safety and well-being. Whether you're exploring the birthplace of Mozart, immersing yourself in the Sound of Music, or savoring the culinary delights, Salzburg promises a blend of tradition and modernity.

As you wander through Mirabell Palace, traverse the Hohensalzburg Fortress, or take in the melodies of classical music, may your time in Salzburg be filled with enchantment and discovery. From the tranquil lakes to the vibrant cultural scenes, every corner of the city invites you to create lasting memories.

Embrace the local etiquette, savor the diverse cuisine, and engage with the warmth of the Salzburgers. Whether you're strolling through the charming Altstadt or embarking on day trips to the surrounding gems, Salzburg welcomes you with open arms.

As you bid farewell to this magical city, may the echoes of its music linger in your heart, and the beauty of its landscapes stay etched in your memories. Safe travels, and may your Salzburg adventure be filled with joy, inspiration, and moments that linger long after you've left its picturesque embrace.

Final Thoughts on Salzburg

Salzburg, a city of timeless beauty and cultural richness, leaves an indelible mark on every visitor. As you conclude your journey in this enchanting Austrian gem, reflect on the experiences that have unfolded against the backdrop of historic architecture, melodious tunes, and breathtaking landscapes.

The city's baroque charm, evident in Mirabell Palace and Gardens, resonates with the spirit of classical music embodied by Wolfgang Amadeus Mozart. The Hohensalzburg Fortress, perched atop the hills, provides not just panoramic views but a glimpse into Salzburg's storied past.

Salzburg's allure extends beyond its cobblestone streets; it's a gateway to natural wonders. The Alps beckon with opportunities for outdoor adventures, while the serene lakes and alpine meadows offer a peaceful retreat.

Dive into the local culture, relishing the culinary delights, exploring the vibrant markets, and partaking in the city's festivals and traditions. The Sound of Music tour evokes cinematic nostalgia, while the warmth of the locals adds a personal touch to your journey.

As you bid adieu to Salzburg, carry with you the echoes of Mozart's melodies, the beauty of the Old Town, and the hospitality of the Salzburgers. May the memories forged during your stay be a source of inspiration, and may the enchantment of Salzburg linger in your heart until you return.

Farewell, and may your travels be filled with the spirit of discovery, cultural richness, and the enduring magic of Salzburg. Safe journeys, and until we meet again in this city of music and dreams.

Your Salzburg Travel Adventure Begins!

Greetings Traveler,

Your esteemed journey through the enchanting city of Salzburg is poised to commence, promising a sojourn marked by cultural opulence, historical grandeur, and natural splendor. As you step into the realm of Mozart's birthplace and the resplendent Hohensalzburg Fortress, prepare to be captivated by the timeless charm woven into the fabric of this Austrian gem.

The baroque magnificence of Mirabell Palace and Gardens shall serve as a prelude to the symphony of classical melodies echoing through the city's illustrious past. With each cobblestone street traversed, you embark on a narrative-rich expedition, delving into the pages of Salzburg's storied history.

Beyond the confines of architectural splendor lies a gateway to nature's wonders. The Alps, with their majestic peaks, extend an invitation to embark on outdoor escapades, while the tranquil lakes and alpine meadows provide a serene haven for contemplation.

Immerse yourself in the rich tapestry of Salzburg's culture. Partake in culinary delights, peruse vibrant markets, and embrace the city's festivals and traditions. The Sound of Music tour, a journey through cinematic nostalgia, and the gracious hospitality of the locals shall render your experience truly memorable.

As you bid adieu to Salzburg, carry with you the harmonious cadence of Mozart's compositions, the architectural allure of the Old Town, and the warmth of Salzburg's inhabitants. May the memories etched during your stay serve as a wellspring of inspiration, and may the enchantment of Salzburg linger in your heart until your eventual return.

Farewell, esteemed traveler, and may your expedition be a harmonious blend of cultural enlightenment, historical immersion, and the enduring magic of Salzburg. Safe travels, until we meet again amidst the melodies and landscapes of this captivating city.

Kind regards,
CARLTON B. MAYNARD

Printed in Great Britain
by Amazon

40281985R00086